the jumbo DUCT TAPE book

book

by Jim and Tim, The Duct Tape Guys
Workman Publishing • New York

Text: Jim Berg, Tim Nyberg, and Tony Dierckins
Design and illustrations: Tim Nyberg
Photography: Tim Nyberg and Erik Saulitis

Library of Congress Cataloging-in-Publication Data

Berg, Jim, 1964–
    The jumbo duct tape book/Jim and Tim.
    p. cm.
    ISBN 0-7611-2110-2 (alk. paper)
    1. Duct tape--Humor. I. Nyberg, Tim, 1953– II. Title.
    PN6231.D79 N936 2001
    818'.5407--dc21   00-043436

Workman books are available at special discounts when purchased in bulk for premiums and sales promotions as well as for fund-raising or educational use. Special editions or book excerpts can also be created to specification. For details, contact the Special Sales Director at the address below.

WORKMAN PUBLISHING COMPANY, INC.
708 Broadway
New York, NY 10003-9555
www.workman.com

Manufactured in the United States of America

First printing September 2000

10 9 8 7 6 5 4 3 2 1

Acknowledgments:

We'd like to thank Duct Tape Pros around the world (you know who you are) for your support and for all the ideas we've pilfered for this book. Thanks to our families and friends who have always been there with their love, ideas, proofreading, constructive criticism, and lots of strong coffee. Thanks to the media, which constantly give us valuable time and space to evangelize "The Gospel of Duct Tape." And a special thanks to Door County, Wisconsin's, electric company — without the power failure of Christmas 1993, none of these duct tape books would exist. To Workman Publishing, which had the benevolent foresight to realize that the world needed to know more about duct tape. And, to Manco, a Henkel Group Company, which keeps our garages filled to the rafters with Duck® brand duct tape.

— Jim and Tim, The Duct Tape Guys

According to the *Chicago Manual of Style* (the standard for the publishing industry), this page is traditionally left blank, but people have always told us that we have no style. So here is page vi (pronounced v'eye) with space for you to jot down your own duct tape notes.

Notes:

Introduction

To those of you who are new to duct tape, you are about to discover a whole new world on a roll. We hope you had the foresight to go out and pick up a roll of duct tape before you started reading so that you can tape along with us. We know that you'll find this book fascinating. In fact, if you stop right now and duct tape your hands to the front and back covers, you'll find this book hard to put down. To Duct Tape Pros who have been with us since 1994, we have accumulated even *more* new duct tape hints but have included some of the best from our previous books and calendars. This is truly *one incredible book!*

Many of the tips in this book are obtained from visitors to our Web site: ***www.ducttapeguys.com.*** We invite you to stop by and see what we've been up to, to share your own unique applications of duct tape with the world, and to see the duct taped fetal pig, Frankenswine (not to be missed).

Disclaimer:

Like our other books, *The Jumbo Duct Tape* Book contains humor. Please don't try any of the hints in this book that are blatantly stupid, potentially injurious, disrespectful to human or animal life, or outright dangerous. Some of the hints are real, usable ideas (we aren't distinguishing which ones). You may want to try some of these or you may not. Whatever the case, you're doing so at your own risk. Other hints are merely for your entertainment (that is, of course, assuming you find extreme stupidity entertaining).

Naturally, all real brand names mentioned in this book are the registered trademarks of their respective owners. Just because they are mentioned here doesn't mean that their companies endorse what we are suggesting.

For best results, we recommend carrying Duck® brand duct tape with you at all times. For worst results, always carry a soldering iron and a tube of processed cheese.

— *Jim and Tim, The Duct Tape Guys*

Rule Number One

This is the rule that can get you through life. If it ain't stuck and it's supposed to be, duct tape it.

Learn Spanish!

On your next trip to Mexico, bring a case of duct tape. Anyone will gladly give you at least a month's room and board and your own private Spanish lessons for your kind gift of duct tape.

Note: Don't drink the water unless you first boil it with a piece of duct tape to catch all the bacteria.

Fastener Fastener

When repairing anything, place the temporarily removed screws, bolts, nuts, and washers on a strip of duct tape so you don't lose them.

"Hey, Jim. Maybe this idea could also help you not lose your marbles!"

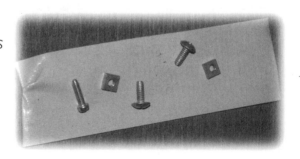

Tree Repair

Storm damage to trees and bushes can often be repaired with duct tape. Duct tape the damaged branch back into place and it will regraft itself. While it secures the limb in place, duct tape also keeps bugs and infection out of the wound.

Of course, if you cover your trees entirely with duct tape from the start, they will be virtually indestructible to begin with.

Volcanic Eruption Protection

To protect yourself from the heat and any stray lava splashes, make sure you are covered with at least 10 layers of duct tape. A shield of sticky-side-out duct tape held in front of you will attract all that volcanic ash, allowing you to breathe freely as you flee town.

Steel Guitar

Turn any ordinary wooden guitar into a "steel guitar" by covering it entirely in duct tape. And what are you going to use for your guitar strap? Duh!

(See Jim's steel guitar on page 205.)

Hang It All!

Do you want to hang your tools on a pegboard, but their handles don't have holes? Just make them a duct tape loop or create a little duct tape tab with a hole punched into it.

Loose Tooth Remover

Dry the surface of your loose tooth
(so the duct tape sticks). Attach one
end of a 12-foot strip of duct tape
to the tooth and the other end to
the back of a drag-racing vehicle.
When the light turns green, your
tooth (and quite possibly the whole
side of your head) will be removed.

You Are Never Lost with Duct Tape

If you're like most guys, you get lost a lot. Duct tape can help! Simply leave a trail of little duct tape squares to help you find your way home again.

Or, duct tape a YOU ARE HERE sign to your chest so you always know where you are.

Duct vs. Duck Tape

Is it *duct* or *duck?* We don't want you to be confused, so we'll explain. The first name for duct tape was "duck." During World War II, the U.S. military needed a waterproof tape to keep moisture out of ammunition cases. They enlisted the Johnson & Johnson Permacel Division to manufacture the tape. Because it was waterproof, everyone referred to it as duck tape (like water off a duck's back). Military personnel discovered that the tape was good for lots more than keeping out water. They used it for jeep repairs, fixing stuff on their guns, strapping equipment to their clothing . . . the list is endless.

After the war, the housing industry was booming and someone discovered that the tape was great for joining heating and air-conditioning ductwork. So the color was changed from army green to the familiar silvery tone of today, and people started to refer to it as duct tape. Therefore, either name is appropriate.

Today, Duck® brand Tape is manufactured by Manco, a Henkel Group Company.

Whether you call it duct tape or duck tape … you are still using the "Ultimate Power Tool" to dramatically improve the quality of your life.

UV Protection

With the depleted
ozone layer, our eyes
are exposed to more
harmful UV radiation.
Play it safe! Get some
of those really big

"old people" sunglasses and cover
them with duct tape — except for
a small slit in the middle.

Pool Shark

Create a little duct tape shark fin and place it on your pool table. Then call attention to it by yelling, "Look! A pool shark!"

Note: You can also use duct tape to repair torn pool-table felt. Place the tape sticky-side-up to make the game even more challenging!

Chaperone Helper

If you suddenly find yourself in charge of chaperoning a bunch of high school kids in a hotel, make sure they stay in their rooms: put a small piece of duct tape between their door and door frame. In the morning, if the tape is loose, broken, or missing, you will know if there were any curfew offenders and who they were.

C·O·U·R·A·G·E

*Even if you have some, it still helps
to have a roll of duct tape on hand.*

Duct Tape

Catch and Release

Practice catch-and-release fishing with minimal damage to the fish — use duct tape instead of a hook. Pull the fish in, peel off the tape, and throw the fish back in the lake.

Presto! Chango!

Change the color of your shoes to match your dress or suit in seconds. Just add colored duct tape.

Or, change the color of your dress or suit to match your shoes. Add some black- or brown-colored duct tape.

Or, just go nude and wear duct tape "fig leaves."

Fizz Keeper

Cover the opening of your carbonated beverage can with duct tape to keep the fizz in until you're ready to finish drinking it.

Variation: If too much soda fizz makes you burp, avoid embarrassment by covering your mouth with duct tape.

Duct Tape
Air Cleaner

Attach strips of duct tape (each about 4 feet long) to every blade of a ceiling fan and turn the fan on "high." The twirling duct tape will suck all the yucky cigar smoke, dead fish smell, and other bad odors onto its super-sticky side as it buffs-n-polishes the air clean with its smooth side.

Italian Rollerblades

Duct tape two pizza cutters to the bottom of each shoe. Mama Mia! You've got yourself some fine Italian Rollerblades.

Note: These work nicely on ice, too.

Name Your Waist Size

Duct tape over the size label on the back of your pants and write in whatever size you wish to be.

Overheard at Jim's 15th high school reunion:

"Jim, are you still a 32-inch waste?!"

Cold Remedy

A strip of duct tape
stuck under your nose
will save you from
the embarrassment
of a drippy nose.

Mustard Plaster

Another cold remedy: Grandma used to recommend a mustard plaster on the chest. The Duct Tape Guys' variation: 12 mustard packets from a fast-food restaurant duct taped to your chest — it's a lot less messy.

Home Video Wall

Duct tape 100 or more television sets together to make a great video wall just like they have at appliance stores. You'll never need to use the remote or miss a favorite show because of a conflict in network scheduling.

Warning: Viewing this much television at one time can result in irreversible drainage of any intelligence you once possessed.

Protect your expensive watch face from getting all scratched up: duct tape over the crystal. You'll make new friends asking for the correct time.

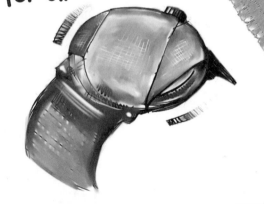

Confidence Builder

Build an ark, just like Noah did —
only build yours entirely out of duct
tape. A big project, to be sure, but
when you're finished, you'll have the
admiration not only of yourself but
also of all those around you.

*"I saw your ark, Tim. It made me think you had
finally gone completely nuts!"*

"Shut up, Jim."

Better Spelling with Duct Tape

For error-proof writing, duct tape a dictionary to your nonwriting arm. If you still happen to make a spelling mistake, you can always use duct tape as white-out on a roll (or gray-out, as the case may be).

Sled Repair

Break your favorite sled? Make sure the sled is bone dry and at room temperature before applying duct tape. Tape overlapping strips from back to front of the entire sled bottom. Better yet, forget the sled and just cover your bottom in duct tape for a built-in sled!

Duct Tape Bandages

Cover your cuts and bruises with as many layers of duct tape as needed to stop the bleeding. Or, use duct tape to secure towels, shirts, blankets, or other forms of compresses on those really nasty wounds.

"We should note, Jim, that we are not doctors, and therefore can't dispense medical advice."

"No problem, Tim. This ain't medical advice, this is just plain common sense first aid."

stump the DUCT TAPE GUYS

Question: A hypothetical problem: I'm in science lab and I throw a beaker of sulfuric acid at the door and make a big hole in it. If I try to put duct tape on the door, the duct tape will just melt. What do I do? — Losdios

Answer: If this should happen, sit in a chair and wrap duct tape around your feet. Then put a strip over your mouth and eyes. Finally, put your hands behind the chair and wrap the tape around your wrists. When the teacher returns to the classroom and finds you, tell him that you were overcome by vandals while doing your lab assignment. This should get you off the hook for the damage to the door. Have your teacher clean up the acid mess — he's trained to do that. — The Duct Tape Guys

E-mail your questions to: tim@ducttapeguys.com

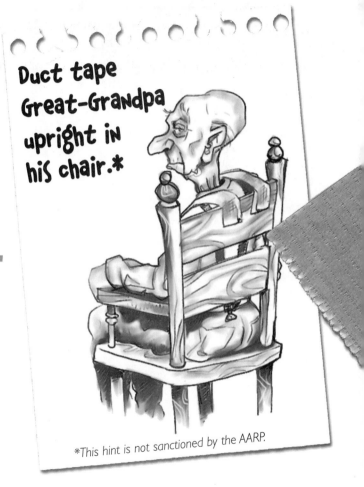

The Duct Tape Sketchbook

Duct tape Great-Grandpa upright in his chair.*

*This hint is not sanctioned by the AARP.

Thanks to the many advertisers who helped make this book possible. When you get the opportunity, visit their businesses and tell them that you saw their ad in *The Jumbo Duct Tape Book*. Or, you could say, "Jim and Tim sent me!" Or, "Hi, my name is [your name],* and I read your ad in Jim and Tim's *Jumbo Duct Tape Book*."

*Where it says "[your name]," simply insert your name — don't say "your name."

Firehouse Practical Joking

Wrap duct tape, sticky-side-out, halfway down the fire pole. Hilarity will ensue when three or four firefighters get jammed up between floors.

Related hint: If you can't find a dalmatian, grab any old dog, cover it with white duct tape, and add little black duct tape dots.

Impromptu Sports

Want to play volleyball but don't have a net? Just fold over a long strip of duct tape and attach it between two trees. No ball? Wad up newspaper and cover it with duct tape. Spike on, dudes!

Protect Those Knees

Forget your knee pads for volleyball? Make new ones with wads of toilet paper or facial tissues covered with duct tape. Plus, if you 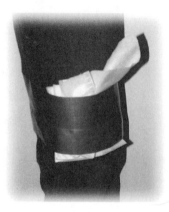 get a runny nose, you can use your knees as a handy tissue dispenser.

Candy Bar Expander

Tired of monkeying around trying to eat those tiny little trick-or-treat candy bars? Duct tape them into one massive candy bar. Eat down to the duct tape, then squeeze!

Candy bar shown before:
and after:

No More Colored Fingers

Dyeing eggs for the annual Easter egg hunt is no longer a messy proposition when you stick the eggs onto a strip of duct tape and dangle them in the dye. Or, skip the dye altogether and cover the eggs with colored duct tape. Heck, for that matter, skip the eggs and just hide rolls of colored duct tape.

An Ounce of Prevention

Cover your goblets and other fine glassware entirely with duct tape so that when they get dropped, they don't shatter all over the floor.

"Tim, I said I was sorry!"

"Be quiet and keep sweeping, Jim!"

Car DeCrumber

Tired of cleaning up the crumbs and cookie chunks in your kid's car seat? Duct tape the whole car seat, sticky-side-out, to catch all that little stuff as it falls.

Butlers: You too can use this hint to decrumb the dining room table. We suggest using black duct tape for a more formal look.

Hinge on a Roll

Break the hinge on the cover of your copier? Fashion a new one with a few strips of duct tape!

Break a hinge on your car door? Duct tape the top edge of the door to the roof of your car and you've got yourself one of them fancy gull-wing doors!

"By the way, Tim, the copier wouldn't have broken if you hadn't been sitting on it!"

Animal-Friendly Fur-Trimmed Clothing

Before your next haircut, lay duct tape, sticky-side-up, over your shoulders. Your falling hair will stick to the tape and create a lovely fur collar that will perfectly match your hair and your complexion.

A Golf Gimme

Can't make those 20-foot putts on your practice green? Duct tape a troughlike lane to the hole. You'll improve ... we guarantee it!

(Illustration shortened from 20 feet due to space limitations)

the DUCT TAPE GUYS™

Stuff from our Secret Recipe File

2 bicycles
+ 1 wheelbarrow
+ 1 umbrella
+ 6 rolls duct tape
_____
= human-powered
golf cart

Avoid Computer Viruses

Lay duct tape, sticky-side-out, on your desk around your computer. We're no computer technologists, but we're pretty sure this will stop any computer bug in its tracks. It worked on our roaches!

Cybersurfing Safety

Prevent your kids from seeing things you don't want them to see as they surf the Web: duct tape over the entire computer screen.

Or, just direct their browser to **www.ducttapeguys.com** *for clean, educational, and fun Web browsing at its finest!*

Keyboarding Aid

If your fingers are too fat to hit the computer keys without hitting the surrounding keys, make "SlimFinger Extenders"™ by duct taping pencils, eraser-side exposed, onto your fingertips.

Bonus hint: If you lost fingers in a shop accident, this hint also works well as a finger replacement device.

The Duct Tape Sketchbook

Suggestion for Letterman and other gap-toothed entertainers:

Before

After

Cruise Control I

A little duct tape
under the gas pedal
and you're
stylin' down
the road with
your own
low-tech
cruise
control.

place wad
of duct tape
under here

Cruise Control II

On those long straightaways —
like when you're driving through
Nebraska — duct tape the steering
wheel to the dashboard, sit back,
and relax. Maybe catch a few winks.

*Note: Neither of these cruise control hints is
endorsed by the National Safety Council, although
we've used them both regularly with only a few
minor mishaps.*

Remote Control Control

Never lose your remote again! Duct tape your television remote control to the arm of your favorite television-watching chair. Or, do what Jim does: duct tape it right to your arm. You'll never again have to relinquish remote control operation to your wife and kids.

Remote Control Control — The Sequel

Too many remotes? Bind them all into one jumbo remote with ... you guessed it, duct tape.

Antifog Device

Prevent the visor on your snowmobile helmet from fogging up. Place a duct tape shield on your nose to deflect the moist exhalation out from under the visor.

exhaust ports out here

No More "Wiggle Legs"

Nervous legs prevent you from getting to sleep at night? Tightly wrap duct tape around each thigh. You'll cut off the circulation so your legs will go numb and won't bother you anymore. (Of course, you may lose your legs if gangrene sets in, but if that happens you won't have to worry about wiggle legs ever again!)

Duct Tape
Space Saver

Tight on space? Use duct tape to
create a wall or ceiling TV mount just
like they have in those fancy sports
bars.

Warning: Make sure you use lots *of duct tape or
you'll be buying your brother-in-law a brand-new
$1200 television set. (Ingrate!)*

Fresh Chips

Duct tape makes a nifty seal to keep your bags of tortilla or potato chips snackin' fresh.

"Also keeps ex-vice president's potatoe chips fresh!"

"Good one, Tim."

"Thanks, Jim."

Hot and Cold Water Mixer

Old houses are great, but those old-fashioned faucets with separate hot and cold taps can be an inconvenience, not to mention a potential burn problem. Duct tape the earpieces of a stethoscope to each spout so that the hot and cold water will blend into a pleasing warm stream.

Ultimate Tool Belt

Build your own Ultimate Tool Belt. Buy one of those fancy leather tool-holder belt contraptions. Hang a roll of duct tape on the tape-holder chain. Fill the remaining pockets with cans of beer.

Impermeable Piñata

After the guest of honor's blindfold is in place, quickly wrap the festive piñata entirely in duct tape. They'll whack at that thing for hours while the rest of you have a good laugh at his/her expense. And instead of filling the piñata with candy, fill it with something people *really* want: rolls of duct tape!

Housebreak Your Dog

Duct tape a kitty litter box to your dog's southern regions. Your pooch will be so humiliated walking around with the litter box attached that it will be eager to learn to use the porcelain fixtures just like you do.

Toothpaste Cap

Constantly losing your toothpaste cap? Make a new

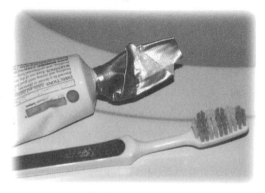

permanent one out of duct tape. Poke a little pinhole in the duct tape and squeeze out a cute little noodle of toothpaste.

Velcro Cleaner

Ever notice that Velcro can get clogged with fuzz? Well, guess what removes that fuzz? That's right! Duct tape. Just dab the sticky side on the Velcro and it will clean up nicely.

"Hey, Tim. Why would anyone bother using Velcro when we have duct tape available?"

"It's just one of the mysteries of life, Jim."

The Duct Tape Sketchbook

Elastic gone from the band of your favorite knee-high stockings? Duct tape them to your leg and they'll stay up all day.

Plus: you won't have to shave your calves!

Lower Your Receding Hairline I

Attach duct tape to your forehead, over your nose, and under your chin. When

Reenactment

you open your mouth, your hairline will return to its normal place.

Key Retriever

Keys lost down the sewer grate? Wrap duct tape, sticky-side-out, around the end of a long stick or broom handle and retrieve them with ease.

Note: If the sewer is running high at the time, we suggest you skip this hint and pop for a locksmith. Jim stunk for three weeks!

Hide-a-Key

Never get locked out of your car
again. Duct tape a key to the rest of
the duct tape that covers the rust on
your rear quarter panel. The only real
trick is remembering which hunk of
duct tape holds the key.

Key Holder

Wad up a bunch of duct tape, sticky-side-out, and put it on your wall. Then stick your keys to the wad.

It's functional and affordable, not to mention highly fashionable wall art.

Convert-a-Car

Convert any car model into a middle-age crisis cruisin' machine. Cut off the roof and with duct tape turn it into a "ragtop" mobile.

But don't stop there! Finish it off with two-tone tuck-n-roll duct tape vinyl upholstery just like those 1950s street rods had.

Duct Taped Tree Treats

Be kind to animals: tape corncobs to trees for birds and squirrels. Or, tape birds and squirrels to trees for dogs and cats.*

*This hint is definitely not endorsed by the ASPCA. In fact, Tim's wife (Jim's sister) and Jim's wife (Tim's sister-in-law) said we should remove this hint. But we figure, hey, it's only a joke. Anyone who would take this hint seriously should be duct taped to the tree right next to the squirrel.

Plate Retainer I

To stop Grandma's decorative plates from sliding off the plate rails, duct tape 'em into place!

Plate Retainer II

To stop Grandpa's upper plate from sliding out of his mouth, duct tape it into place!

No more birdseed and feathers on the floor under your birdcage. Just put duct tape walls half-way up the cage.

The Duct Tape Sketchbook

Buddy Rich Wannabe Helper

Drummers: To keep from losing your sticks during those wild solos, duct tape them to your hands.

Go a little bit too wild? Duct tape your drum heads back together.

Go really wild? Make a duct tape neck brace until your whiplash goes away.

the DUCT TAPE GUYS™

Stuff from our Secret Recipe File

Duct tape
+ magic marker
= label maker

Driveway Sealer on a Roll

Avoid summertime scam artists: seal-coat your driveway yourself with 100 percent pure duct tape. Nothing says "high-class residence" like an oil- and stain-resistant solid silver duct tape driveway.

Trolling with Duct Tape

Give ice fishing a whole new twist:
duct tape a chain saw to the front of
your fishing boat and troll all year long.
Or, hook up your ice house to the
back of your pickup, duct tape the
chain saw to the trailer hitch, put the
truck in gear, and do your trolling in
the warmth of your fishing shanty.

No Double-Dipping

Get your fill of dip on every bite while avoiding double-dipping. Make a little duct tape scoop and use it to apply dip to your chips.

Duct Tape Trench Coat

Turn your short jacket into a butt-covering trench coat. Add to its length and durability with strips of matching or complementary-colored duct tape.

Cookout Combo

Duct tape a burger flipper and
a flyswatter handle-to-handle
for the ultimate in convenient
cookout insect control.

Dress Code Helper

If you go to one of those fancy-pants restaurants and forget your necktie, just take out your roll of duct tape and create a spill-resistant necktie that will match any sport coat.

Forget your sport coat, too? Duct tape over the maître d's eyes while he's seating you.

Auto Booster Seat

Short drivers can raise themselves by duct taping several old telephone books to the driver's seat.

Optional hint: Tape the phone books right to your butt so you get a lift wherever you sit.

Still too short? Move to a city with a bigger phone book.

Pill Minder

If you have to remember to take a bunch of pills each day, fasten your daily dosage onto a piece of duct tape attached to the mirror above your bathroom sink. One glance and you'll see if you forgot to take any pills.

On the go? Fasten the Pill Minder onto your forehead. You'll remember your pills whenever you look in a mirror.

Built-In Magazine Rack

Put strips of folded-over duct tape across the opening of any unused door to hang your magazines just like libraries do on those racks.

Postal Protection

Prevent dog bites by making bite-proof multilayered duct tape leggings. For really big dogs, you might want to consider the Total Body Armor described on page 92 of this book.

Car CD Caddie

Duct tape your sun visor sticky-side-out and attach your CDs to it (label-side to the tape). If the sun is sneaking around the visor, add more CDs.

Glove Compartment Latch Replacement

Older cars sometimes have weak or nonexistent glove compartment latches. Duct tape creates a strong yet removable solution for this closure problem.

No glove compartment? Duct tape your stuff to the dashboard.

Cheap Briefcase

Public assistance lawyers: Make a briefcase by duct taping over a pizza delivery box.
Add a duct tape handle and latch if you wish.

Make a Treepod

No need to carry a tripod when you're backpacking. Duct tape your camera to a tree for those group shots.

Bonus hint: For that Blair Witch *"wiggle-cam," duct tape your video camera to your leg and run through the woods. This would be called a "legpod."*

Construction Worker Softball

Play an impromptu softball game during your lunch break using a wadded-up piece of duct tape as the ball and a duct taped two-by-four for a bat.

Speaking of construction workers ... remember that guy who used superglue to fasten his hard hat to an I-beam? Well, if he'd used duct tape, he'd still be hanging there!

Tax Prep and Duct Tape

When you've finished preparing your tax return, super-seal the envelope with a few layers of duct tape (increase the number of layers in accordance with the amount of money you owe). Then you can use duct tape to patch that hole your fist made in the wall.

stump the DUCT TAPE GUYS

Question: As you know, seat belts are required by law. Mine fell apart, so I made a new one out of duct tape. A policeman noticed it and gave me a ticket. How can duct tape help me get my ticket excused so I don't pay the fine or have the violation on my record? — Terry K.

Answer: Take the dude to court and challenge him to a side-by-side comparison of *your* duct tape seat belt against the original factory-installed belts. If your car is old enough, it will become apparent that the duct tape belt is stronger than the aged fabric belts; therefore, you're even safer than with a conventional belt. Make sure your belt is composed of at least six layers of duct tape and it should be no contest! — *The Duct Tape Guys*

E-mail your questions to: tim@ducttapeguys.com

Magnetic Therapy

In pain? Don't buy one of those trendy and expensive homeopathic magnet belts! You can achieve the same results by duct taping magnets to your aching back and joints.

Do-It-Yourself Total Body Armor

Duct tape and scrap iron combine to make effective and inexpensive armor for the whole body. Perfect if you happen to be making one of those postapocalyptic films.

Warning: Don't get too close to someone using the hint on the previous page!

the DUCT TAPE GUYS™

Stuff from our Secret Recipe File

Recipe for homemade duct tape:

1. Seventy-five feet strong but easily ripped two-inch-wide cloth.

2. One can really sticky adhesive.

3. One can "pewter" spray paint.

Mix well and use with pride!

Stay in the Saddle!

You'll be able to stay on the wildest horse in the rodeo when you duct tape yourself to the saddle! And to avoid saddle sores, duct tape a pillow to your rear end.

Bonus hint: When calf roping, secure the calf's calves with duct tape. You won't need to spend time learning them fancy cowboy knots.

Follow the Yellow Brick Road

For your next *Wizard of Oz* viewing party, make a yellow brick road out of yellow duct tape to lead your guests to your front door. And remember, cardboard covered with classic gray duct tape creates a nifty Tin Man costume.

Mailing Tubes

Save those old toilet-paper and paper-towel rolls and duct tape them together end-to-end to make mailing tubes. Save enough of them and you won't need the postal service anymore — just line up the tubes between your house and Grandma's house, hook a vacuum cleaner to each end, and you have a pneumatic mailing system.

Bearing Good News

Wheel bearings go out? Repacking the bearings with duct tape will get you to the nearest garage.

"Jim, I thought you told me you greased the wheel bearings!"

"No, I said my stomach couldn't bear eating any more of that really greasy food!"

"Well, thank God for duct tape or we'd still be sittin' in the middle of that desert!"

Operation Duct Hook

Aircraft carrier commanders could stop throwing money away on the arresting lines and tail hooks used to help stop landing jets if they would just cover the flight deck with duct tape, sticky-side-up.

The Duct Tape Sketchbook

use yellow duct tape to make fake dotted centerlines to trick people into driving off cliffs just like they do in the cartoons.*

*This hint is not recommended by the National Safety Council, but it's used frequently by the National Guild of Animators.

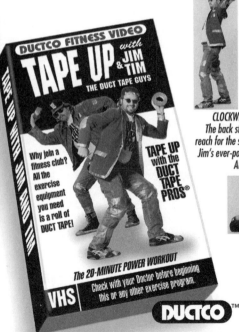

Splinter Preventer

Put a strip of duct tape on both sides of the piece of wood you're about to cut and it won't splinter out.

"That's a good idea, Tim. But you know what I do to avoid splintering wood? I just duct tape over the cut end and it gives the cut a smooth, silvery finish."

"Excellent suggestion, Jim."

Duct Tape Removes Bee Stingers

A Las Vegas woman who was stung 500 times by a swarm of killer bees had the stingers removed by hospital personnel using tweezers and duct tape. Really. Now, if she had only been covered head-to-toe with duct tape from the start, this painful procedure wouldn't have been necessary. Live and learn!

Plug Bee Holes

Speaking of bees, are bees or wasps nesting in your house siding? Just put a small duct tape plug into the entrance hole and cover it with a couple of strips of duct tape. The bees will move to a spot that features easier access to their living quarters.

This concludes the "Bee Section" of our book. Go eat some honey.

Morning After Rehearsal Dinner Helper

So you suddenly find yourself having to make a speech at a wedding, but you're still suffering from the fun you had at the rehearsal dinner? Just duct tape your eyelids open and an ice pack to your aching head.

Clever Clubs

Golfers: Why carry all those clubs when duct tape and simple math can lighten your load?* With just 2 through 5 irons, you can create the rest. Follow this handy chart:

6 iron = Duct tape the 4 & 2 together
7 = 5 & 2 or 4 & 3
8 = 5 & 3
9 = 5 & 4

*The fewer clubs in your bag, the easier it is to carry more beer!

Pewter Flatware

Prevent your silverware from tarnishing: cover it entirely in duct tape. It'll look like a fine set of antique pewter flatware.

Or, duct tape over plastic flatware. Add some lead fishing sinkers under the tape to give it the weight of real pewter.

(See page 352 for matching plates.)

Understated Bumper Sticker

Use a strip of duct tape as a bumper sticker. No need for a slogan — the duct tape will speak for itself.

Diaper Dilemmas Solved with Duct Tape

1. Toddler keep taking diaper off? Duct tape it on!
2. Check diaper and it's dry? Use duct tape to reseal the tabs.
3. Run out of diapers? Duct tape the baby's openings until you can run to the store for more diapers.*

*Not recommended unless you want to become acquainted with the local social service agency.

the DUCT TAPE GUYS™

Stuff from our Secret Recipe File

Recipe for Jim and Tim's
Homemade Disposable Diapers:
Three to nine layers of paper
toweling wrapped around baby's
bottom covered with duct tape.
(Holds thirty to forty pounds.)

Amusement Park Money Saver

When you're going on those topsy-turvy carnival rides, duct tape your pockets shut so you don't lose any pocket change and end up paying extra for the ride.

Do-It-Yourself Amusement Park

Create your own amusement park ride. Duct tape your lawn tractor's steering wheel so it goes in a circle. Attach a wagon, load up the kids, start the engine, and put it in gear. They'll soon experience the same nausea as if you'd paid big bucks at the amusement park.

Motel/Hotel Hints

Always have duct tape in your suitcase so you can utilize these handy travel hints.

1. A folded-over strip of duct tape hanging from wall to wall over your hotel room bathtub makes a great temporary clothesline.

2. Fire in the hallway? Duct tape around the door to keep the smoke out of your room.

3. Duct tape over your window to prevent the flashing MOT L sign from keeping you awake.

4. A strip of duct tape dangling from the bathroom faucet into the sink bowl prevents that sleep-disturbing dripping.

5. No refrigerator in your room? Duct tape your beverage container in front of the air conditioner.

Ecologically Responsible Flushing

Save water by duct taping your old beer bottles and milk jugs to the inside walls of your toilet tank.
It will take less water to fill the tank — and therefore less water is used for each flush.

Note: This new system may require three or four flushes to empty the bowl.

Home Brew Helper

Use duct tape to label
your bottles of home
brew. Or, if you're too lazy
to brew your own, duct
tape over the labels of
beer bottles and pass
them off as your own
home brew.

Auto Trim on a Roll

Vinyl trim falling off your Volare wagon?
Cover it in a duct tape color that
complements the rust tone of your
side panels. Don't stop there! Duct
tape over your rear windows to create
limousine-like privacy.

Now Showing

Theater owners:
Do the letters keep
falling off your marquee?
Prevent STAR WARS from
becoming TAR WA S by
duct taping the movie
titles into place. Replace missing
letters with your own self-adhering
duct tape letters.

Join the Xtreme Sports Set

Duct tape your old ski boots to an ironing board and the next thing you know, you're snowboardin', dude!

Malibu variation: Duct tape your flip-flops to the bottom of an ironing board and catch a wave!

Biker's Buddy

If you're biking and have a flat, duct tape makes an excellent substitute tube patch.

"Heck, just do what Jim and I do. Remove the tire and wrap each rim with forty-three layers of industrial-quality duct tape."

"Yeah, they won't go flat because they're flat to begin with!"

Static-Free Reception

Duct tape a few of those antistatic dryer sheets to your television antenna to provide static-free

reception. They'll also make your television room smell springtime fresh.

Dollhouse Helper

Decorating a dollhouse? Get out your roll of duct tape to:

1. Make classy gray wallpaper.
2. Cover a tongue depressor to make a little doll slide.
3. Make or repair roof shingles.
4. Create "solar roof panels."
5. "Pave" the driveway (we recommend black duct tape).
6. Create wall mirrors.

7. Make a self-adhering tablecloth.
8. Make little area rugs to cover the dollhouse floors.
9. Help the dolls stand in place.
10. Make awnings, etc.

"How do you make 'etc.' with duct tape, Tim?"

"Don't ask stupid questions, Jim."

Body Shop on a Roll

Have a roll or two of duct tape in your vehicle at all times — you never know when you're going to need to reattach a rear quarter panel or something. And, when you're not using it to fix something, place the roll up on your dashboard — the center of the roll makes an excellent beer can holder.

Dieting Tip

Duct tape the light button on the refrigerator so the light doesn't go on when you open the door. It makes the food less appealing and, therefore, quite resistible.

Note: If you're not dieting but you have food like ours that's old and furry, you too will appreciate not being able to see it.

Budget Electric Car

If you can afford a large child's wagon and four cordless drills, you can afford an electric car.

1. Remove wagon wheels.
2. Replace axles with large screws.
3. Place screw heads into drill chucks.
4. Duct tape drills to bottom of wagon so wheels are back in place.
5. Switch drill direction on right-side drills to "reverse."
6. Turn on drills.
7. Drive!

The Duct Tape Sketchbook

Improve your batting average:

Duct Tape small statuary to your batting helmet.

This distracts the pitcher.

Note: Nudes work best.

Limo on a Roll

Duct tape a wall of cardboard behind the driver's seat of your car — just like the limos have. It gives your backseat passengers limo-like privacy, and you can avoid the problem of the kids in the backseat dumping their juice boxes down your back.

stump the DUCT TAPE GUYS

Question: *My neighbor's dog has telepathic powers. It keeps on barking in my head! I would normally duct tape its mouth shut, but since the dog is only barking in my head, I can't. Help! This dog is keeping me up all night!* — Mac

Answer: Since the barking is only in your head, you must merely *think* about duct taping the dog's mouth shut. This will solve the problem. — *The Duct Tape Guys*

E-mail your questions to:
tim@ducttapeguys.com

Improve Your Grades

Kids: Turn an F into a B! Rip little strips of duct tape the width of the pen line in the grade book. Put one short strip coming out at a right angle from the bottom of the F and another strip going vertically from the bottom of the previous strip to the top line of the top right of the F. Congratulations! You're now on the honor roll.

Deer hunters:
Duct tape and a lawn chair makes a cheap and comfortable tree stand. For safety, cover your seat and clothing in blaze orange duct tape.

What's That Sound?!

Duct tape a long
strip of bubble wrap
to your friend's car
tires. When they
drive away, they'll
think something's

wrong with their car. (Or that
somebody is shooting at them with
an automatic weapon, depending on
the neighborhood they live in.)

Urban Camouflage

If you cover yourself in duct tape, you will virtually disappear in most downtown construction areas due to the proliferation of duct tape use. If you're really skinny and use this hint, you'll blend right into the scaffolding posts.

Foot Soak

Soak and soothe your sore feet all day long. Duct tape a plastic garbage bag filled with water onto each foot.

Here, Rover!

Lost your pooch?

Duct tape a pork chop to your chin.

Your dog will find you.

"Tim, you might want to tell them that when you tried this hint, you had eleven dogs pounce on you. They darn near licked your beard right off!"

"Thanks a lot, Jim! I was trying to forget that horrible incident . . . disregard this hint."

Gift Bag on a Roll

Need to wrap a gift quickly? Those trendy little gift bags are a good idea, but they can cost a pretty penny! Create your own gift bag that is both lovely and durable, yet also inexpensive. Cover a paper bag with duct tape, attach duct tape handles, insert your gift, and you're good to go!

Landscaper's Back Saver

No longer do you need to lift those backbreaking and expensive decorative boulders to beautify your yard. Just wad up old newspapers and cover them with duct tape. Soon your yard will be filled with lightweight, durable, and waterproof duct tape boulders.

Stash Your Valuables

Hide your valuables from burglars
by duct taping them out of sight
(say, under tables and chairs).

*Warning: If your burglar happens to be a Duct Tape
Pro, this hint might backfire — as they may sniff out
the duct tape.*

the DUCT TAPE GUYS

Homemade Duct Tape Rope

Duct tape your electric drill onto a firm surface. Wrap some duct tape around the drill bit, but don't rip the tape off the roll. Unwind the roll as far as you want, then turn on the drill. The spinning action will twist your duct tape into a super-strong rope.

Cutting-Edge Cutlery Tips

1. Cover your knife blades in duct tape to keep them sharp when not in use.
2. Turn any knife into a butter knife. Duct tape over the sharp edge.
3. Turn any knife into a Swiss Army knife by duct taping spoons, forks, screwdrivers, toothpicks, corkscrews, etc. onto the handle.

Pet Podiatrist

If your dog or cat has a ripped pad on the bottom of its paw, make a little duct tape booty to protect the wound while it heals.

Budget Zamboni

Make ice-rink resurfacing fast and easy! Duct tape a bunch of damp mops to the back of your compact car and take a few turns around the neighborhood ice-skating rink.

Note: Keep your car moving or the mops will freeze to the ice and rip off your back bumper.

Reattaching Your Car Bumper

1. Purchase three rolls of duct tape.
2. Align bumper in its former location.
3. Apply a 3-foot strip of tape from each of the vehicle's side panels to each end of the bumper.
4. Use the remaining tape to secure the bumper to anything that doesn't move.

Fan Belt Replacement

Blow a fan belt in the desert?
Do what hundreds have
already successfully done:
braid three doubled-over
strips of duct tape into
a replacement belt
and drive on to your
destination!

Become a Marathon Winner!

Share top honors at the next Boston Marathon! Duct tape yourself to the side of the lead camera vehicle. Just before you reach the end of the course, untape yourself and stride effortlessly across the finish line.

One-Person Rowing Team

Duct tape all the oars in an eight-person rowing boat to two long boards. Duct tape your hands to the center of each board and you can drive the thing all by yourself.

"By the way, Tim, next time it's my turn to stand in the front and yell at you."

Duct tape two turtles shell-to-shell so if they accidentally get flipped over, they can still get where they're going.*

*Not endorsed by the ASPCA.

Screw Starter

Avoid risking high blood pressure when trying to get a small screw into a tight space. Just duct tape the screw to the end of your screwdriver to help get it started.

Duct tape here holds screw for you

Small-Pet Retrieval

If your small pet (snake, turtle, hamster, rat, etc.) gets loose in the house, lay out strips of duct tape sticky-side-up. The critter will be caught in no time.

"By the way, Jim, I think I found your hamster."

"Great! Where's my little Fluffy?"

"See that lump in the snake over there?"

Hurricane Helper

Use duct tape to prevent water from coming in around doors and windows during hurricanes. Duct tape the cracks around the perimeter of each door and window. Your roof may blow off, but your doors and windows will hold fast!

stump the DUCT TAPE GUYS

Question: *My house is burning down! How can I use duct tape to stop the raging fire? — NetMaster7@ ...*

Answer: Obviously, by the time we got your e-mail the house was already burned to the ground. Next time, use your head and call 911 or the fire department. Don't be asking a couple of yahoos like us for advice.
— *The Duct Tape Guys*

E-mail your questions to:
tim@ducttapeguys.com

Front Step Friend Catcher

Lonesome? No friends? Get duct tape! Place it sticky-side-out on your front steps and soon you'll have plenty of folks to visit with: postal carriers, window replacement salesmen, religious witnesses, and the occasional Girl Scout.

Birdie Treat

Spill some birdseed on
your kitchen counter,
then pick it up with
the sticky side of
a strip of duct tape.
Now hang the strip

of duct tape from a tree branch or the
eaves of your house as a treat for your
feathered friends.

Gulf War Budget Helper

During Desert Storm, helicopter blades eroded from the sand. A smart technician saved the government thousands of dollars by covering the portion of the blades most vulnerable to damage with duct tape. When the tape wore off, it was simply replaced with a new strip. Now *that's* military intelligence!

Drip Detour

Keep sweat out of your eyes: use duct tape to create a cute little gutter for your forehead.

Tailgater Deterrent

Duct tape a large mirror to the back of your car. In daylight, the blinding glare from the sun will keep other drivers back. At night, the reflection of their own headlights will hold them at bay.

Swamp Cruiser

Combine duct tape, a chair, some old water skis, and an electric fan with a really long extension cord, and you're cruisin' the swamps in your own Everglade Cruiser!

Warning: There is a pretty good chance that this hint poses a severe electrocution hazard.

Secure the Perimeter

Police officers: Use duct tape to secure a crime area instead of that flimsy yellow plastic tape. You'll have a better chance of keeping unauthorized people out.

Gray-Wall Tires

Want to really turn heads on the
road? Upgrade your ride by adding
duct tape to the sidewalls of your plain
black tires.

Burglar Binder

Misplace the keys to your handcuffs? Nothing is quite as effective as duct tape for securing criminals until the police arrive.

"Jim, did you know that the L.A. police used duct tape handcuffs during the riots?"

"That's old news, Tim."

Kitchen Table Saw

Use your circular saw to cut a slit in the top of your kitchen table. Then use plenty of duct tape to mount that same saw under the table so that the blade comes up through the slit. There, wasn't that easy? You just made yourself a table saw!

Learn Ventriloquism at Home — Fast!

Duct tape over your dummy's mouth and mumble your words (as if you have a strip of duct tape over  your mouth). It's very convincing, and you'll make no telltale lip movements!

Ensure-a-Smile

Retail employees and waitpersons: Don't feel like smiling? Stretch duct tape from each side of your mouth around to the back of your head for a perma-smile. (We're pretty sure this hint is being successfully implemented by some televangelists.)

Pickpocket Protection

Duct tape your wallet securely into your pocket. Or, skip the wallet and just duct tape your money onto your belly under your shirt.

Warning: Hair removal imminent.

Riverdance Pro

Perfect your Irish dancing technique: duct tape your arms to your sides.

Tether Your Board, Dudes!

Surfers and snowboard enthusiasts: Tether your board to your leg with doubled-over duct tape.

Worried about going off a cliff? Quickly tether yourself to the nearest tree.

Whole-Body Splint

Take a nasty multiple-bone-breaking tumble while snowboarding or skiing? Don't wait for the National Ski Patrol — simply duct tape a 4-by-8-foot sheet of plywood to the front of your body, and one to the back. Then slide yourself down the hill to the hospital.

Don't Mess with the Thermostat!

Dads: Keep the thermostat set where you want it. Duct tape it into place.

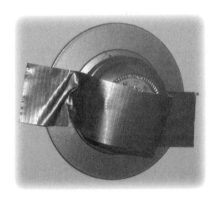

Redirect Heat Flow

Kids: Has Dad duct taped the thermostat at a constant 67°F and it's cold in your room? Use duct tape to seal off heating ducts in all rooms but yours; this will reroute all the heat to you.

stump the DUCT TAPE GUYS

Problem: *My cat is stupid.* — *SPAMM34@ . . .*

Answer: Don't worry. This is not a problem. There is nothing wrong with your cat. As far as we have been able to tell, all cats are stupid. Either that or they are extremely smart and just act like complete, brainless idiots so that nothing is expected of them. So how can duct tape help your cat "problem"? Well, if you duct tape your cat to the ceiling, you will elevate your cat's intelligence. While your cat is duct taped to the ceiling, go out and buy a dog. — *The Duct Tape Guys*

E-mail your questions to:
tim@ducttapeguys.com

No Ears?

Duct tape your eyeglasses to your head.

No Nose?

Duct tape your eyeglasses to your head.

No Eyes?

Skip this page.

EMT Helper

Paramedics: Duct tape your accident victims to the stretcher so they don't accidentally roll off and bounce down a 40-foot embankment when you're trying to load them into the ambulance.

"Jim, it's no wonder that your career as an EMT lasted about four hours."

"I'm still bitter about that one, Tim."

Plumber's Helper

Fold duct tape strips over onto themselves to make little slings to hold water pipes in new construction. Nail the duct tape ends to the floor joists and the pipe will be securely in place. It's cheaper than metal pipe hangers and works just as well.

Moving-Day Hint

Running low on boxes? Leave your stuff in dressers, nightstands, desks, etc., and duct tape the drawers in place for transport. Unpacking is as easy as removing the duct tape!

Create-a-Pew

Create your own church pew: duct tape folding chairs together leg-to-leg. Then tape Bibles and hymnals to the seat backs.

Boring Sermons?

Duct tape parishioners upright in your Create-a-Pew.

No More Head Banging

When working under the car, duct tape a foam pillow to your forehead to prevent gashes and brain injuries when you inevitably bump your head.

Biking Shorts

Lycra becomes almost obsolete once you discover that you can cover any old pair of shorts with shiny, waterproof duct tape.

Warning: Applying duct tape directly to your hip and leg region can result in some painful sticky-side effects.

Computer Security

Duct tape your computer to your desk so it doesn't vibrate off in the next earthquake. Also, secure your mouse cord to the top of the desk with a strip of duct tape so you have to think twice before flinging it at your coworkers.

Duct Tape Is Next to Godliness

Make a durable cover for your Bible (and other important books) with durable, waterproof duct tape. You can use multiple colors for decoration and personalization.

"Jim, do you think there will be duct tape in heaven?"

"Well, if there isn't, it was probably just an oversight on God's part. Once we bring it to His attention, I'm sure He'll get us some."

Space Jerky

Forget to buy Halloween candy for the trick-or-treaters? Quickly tear duct tape into 6-inch strips, twist, and tell the kids it's "Space Jerky."

Space Jerky!

No calories! No cholesterol! No flavor!

Bungee Helper

Eliminate dangerously sharp tips of
bungee-cord hooks with a protective
coating of duct tape. Better yet, eliminate the need for bungee cords —
just stick your stuff to your other
stuff using duct tape.

Wedding Album Gray-Out

Why throw away perfectly good wedding photographs just because your marriage went south? Use strategically placed strips of duct tape to cover up images of your ex.

Lounge Chair Luge

For a more relaxing day of skiing, duct tape skis to the bottom of your favorite easy chair and hit the slopes.

Starving Artist Helper

Painters: There's no longer a need for expensive easels. Duct tape your canvases to the nearest wall and start painting. (Of course, there's really no need for messy paint, either, now that duct tape comes in a variety of colors!)

Instrumental Protection

Musicians: Those flimsy instrument cases are made durable and waterproof, not to mention really good looking, when you cover them entirely in duct tape.

"Hey, Tim. This hint would also be great for budget-strapped mafioso and gangsters who can't afford new violin cases for their weapons."

"Don't get mixed up with that element, Jim."

Potty Training

Use duct tape as the reward for
going "big boy/girl potty!" Have a roll
of duct tape and a little chart in the
bathroom next to your child's potty
chair. Whenever he/she makes an
effort to go potty, give him/her a little
square of duct tape to put on the
chart. If he/she goes number two,
give him/her *two* squares! He/she
will be potty trained in no time.

Driveway Snow Removal

Why hire a snowplow when you can do it yourself by duct taping a bunch of shovels to your car's front bumper?

Better yet, make a huge duct tape car tunnel leading from the street into your garage and the snow will never get onto your driveway in the first place.

Red Means Stop!

Go-cart track owners: Put a strip of red duct tape on each cart's brake pedal to help kids find it when it's time to stop. If that doesn't work, you can always patch the fence with duct tape.

Super Kite

No more ripped kites when you make them with duct tape instead of that flimsy tissue paper. Sure, it may take gale-force winds to keep them aloft, but there probably won't be any other kite fliers competing for sky space.

Duct tape string and tail, also!

Formal on a Roll

With a roll of black duct tape and an old jacket, you've got yourself a swallow-tail tux. Have a roll of white duct tape? You've got yourself a starched shirtfront. Get that black roll out again and make yourself a bow tie and tummy-holding cummerbund. See how easy it is to save money and look great with duct tape?

No More Rented Shoes

Don't rent shoes to go with your tux — simply purchase a pair of shoes to go with your formalwear. Duct tape over the shoe bottoms so they don't get scuffed, then remove the duct tape and return the shoes* for full credit when the event is over.

*Not endorsed by the National Shoe Retailers Association.

Power-Window Problems

If your car's power window refuses to close automatically, attach a strip of duct tape to the top edge of the glass so you can manually pull it closed. Then duct tape it into place until you want to lower it again.

"Or do what Jim did ... break all your car windows and tape over the openings until you need a breeze."

The Duct Tape Sketchbook

Cell Phone Safety

Don't be stupid. If you need to talk on the cell phone in your car, play it safe! Duct tape the phone to your head and keep both hands firmly on the wheel.

This has been a public service announcement from Jim and Tim, The Duct Tape Guys.

Bandage Fastener

Secure bandages with duct tape for more durability in wet conditions. And Ace bandages can be fastened with duct tape if you lose that little clip thingee.

"With duct tape, why would anyone need an Ace bandage, Tim?"

"Some people aren't as advanced as you, Jim."

Roadkill Relocator

Don't want to touch that gunky squirrel that got flattened in front of your driveway? We don't blame you. Just duct tape your tires, sticky-side-out, and drive over it as you continue on your way. It will redeposit itself down the road in front of your neighbor's driveway.

Cat Scratch Reliever

Cat clawing the furniture? One family duct taped their cat to the offended couch leg for two hours. The cat hasn't returned to the couch since.

Rah! Rah! Raccoon Coat!

Duct tape live raccoons to your coat. This makes an impressive fashion statement without risking harassment from those antifur activists — they wouldn't dare spray-paint a *live* raccoon coat!

Gas Cap Replacement

Lose your gas cap? Stuff a sock in the filler tube and duct tape the filler door shut to prevent the gas fumes from escaping. After a couple of weeks, remove the sock and use it to start your barbecue coals.*

Warning: Stand back six feet when igniting the sock! Duct tape your match to the end of a long stick.

Duct Tape your face to a pan filled with water and smelly herbal/medicinal stuff. Set the pan on a hot burner and inhale the steam for a nice facial.

Blade Guard

When disposing of used X-Acto and utility knife blades, cover them with duct tape to avoid ripped garbage bags and cuts to your garbage handler. If the garbage guy does happen to sever a finger, be available with your roll of duct tape to fasten it back onto his hand.

Sharp blade + duct tape sheath = less of this

Jigsaw Puzzle Saver

After you finish a massive jigsaw puzzle, preserve it and show off your accomplishment: duct tape the back of the puzzle so you can hang it on the wall.

Helpful hint: Build your puzzle on a table that is covered with sticky-side-up duct tape and your puzzle will be pretaped when you finish! And when it gets bumped, your hours of hard work won't fly all over the room.

"I said I was sorry, Tim . . ."

Coffee Cup Keeper

Never misplace your coffee cup again: duct tape it onto your hand.

Gutter Unclogger

To prevent your gutters from becoming clogged with leaves, duct tape over them. Rainwater will roll gently onto the ground.

Or, simply duct tape all your leaves onto the tree branches so they won't fall in the first place.

Strike Up the Band!

1. Duct tape the top of a pan, barrel, or oatmeal container; you've got yourself a drum.

2. Duct tape a funnel to a hose; you've got yourself a newfangled horn.

3. Duct tape a broomstick to the side of an upside-down washtub. Fold four feet of duct tape onto itself lengthwise; attach one end to the top of the broom handle and the other to the middle of the washtub. Voilà! You've got yourself a gut bucket.

4. And, of course, the sound of pulling duct tape from the roll is music to anyone's ears!

Jim and Tim's instruments of choice are a Harmonicarp,
a hybrid of a harmonica and a freshwater carp (the results
of a nasty lab accident), and a steel guitar (which Jim made
by duct taping his shrunken wooden guitar).

Fiberglass Sliver Remover

Use duct tape to remove those itchy
little slivers the next time you work
with fiberglass insulation. Or, practice
"an ounce of prevention" by sheathing
your arms in duct tape prior to
touching the material.*

Obviously, this hint creates hair-bare arms.

P·R·I·D·E

It comes free with every roll of duct tape.

Duct Tape

Mirror Ball Mania

Duct tape chunks of a broken mirror to an old basketball, hang it from the ceiling, spin it, hit it with a flashlight, and you're ready to disco!

Or, make a human mirror ball: duct tape mirror chunks to the largest guy on the dance floor and shine a spotlight on him when he's dancing.

Duct Tape Creates Stronger Trees

Protect young trees while they establish themselves. Duct taping their trunks protects them from pests and disease.

Travel Spill Preventer

Duct tape the tops onto your travel shampoo, conditioner, lotions, and perfume bottles to avoid a surprise when you open up your suitcase.

"Tim, someone squirted shampoo all over my clothes!"

"It was high time you washed them anyway, Jim."

The Duct Tape Sketchbook

Achieve that Vegas-era Elvis look by duct taping the lapels of an old sport coat. And black duct tape makes great Elvis muttonchops.

Suitcase Locator

Your luggage is easily spotted at any airport baggage claim when you have a large duct tape X on each side.

Or, cover your entire suitcase in duct tape — it will be virtually indestructible. And talk about easy to spot ..!

Hot Dish Holder

When you bring
your casserole to
a potluck dinner,
enclose the bowl
in newspaper and

wrap it with duct tape. Your clever
Hot Dish Holder may receive more
compliments than your recipe!

Duct Tape Doggy Door

In the bottom of your door, cut a hole large enough to accommodate your dog. Overlap strips of doubled duct tape over the door to prevent breezes. Make the sticky side of the strips face the outside and they'll groom loose hair, burrs, and other unwanted items from your dog's fur as it enters the house.

Blister Buffer

Got a nagging blister from shoes that are ill fitting? Duct tape over the blister area and you'll find quick relief.

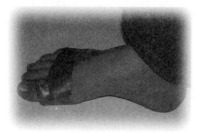

"Jim, time to clip those toenails!"

"Nah, I'll just tape over them."

Laser Cat Tag Games

Lay little strips of duct tape sticky-side-up around your living room. Then get out your laser pen and let your cat chase the red dot around the room. Hilarity ensues when the cat hits the duct tape "land mines."

Duct Tape Shelving

Cover cheap particleboard with
duct tape to make an ultramodern
metallic shelving unit. For the
supports, use spare rolls of duct
tape. Or, you can
hang the shelves
from the ceiling
using the duct
tape sling method.

The duct tape
sling method

Gaffer's Tape vs. Duct Tape

What's the difference between gaffer's (gaff) tape and duct tape, you ask? Gaffer's tape is made specifically for taping down cables on floors and is meant to be removed. The adhesive is therefore not as tacky as duct tape's. Because it's often used for theater and concert applications, gaffer's tape is usually flat black to avoid reflection. Duct tape will leave a residue (removable with adhesive removers) when it's removed from surfaces.

Pool Cue Case

Save up your empty toilet-paper tubes, join them end-to-end, and encase them in a silvery skin of duct tape. You'll be carrying your prized pool cue in style.

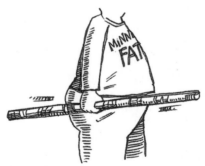

Reflexology on a Roll

Duct tape marbles firmly into place on your body's pressure points. You will be living pain-free in no time.

Note from Tim:
Jim seems to be pretty much pain-free, but I don't think it has anything to do with reflexology. It has something to do with the connective tissue in his brain. I wonder if duct tape can fix that?

Hide-a-Hangnail

Prevent your hangnails from catching on everything — cover them with duct tape. This will not only protect your "owwees" but also allow you to fit in perfectly with your local heavy metal band's manicurist.

No Parking?
No Problem.

Can't find a parking space? Just pull into a yellow curb (no parking) area and cover the curb with white or gray duct tape.

Bonus hint: If you do get a ticket, use a roll of duct tape to bribe the judge.

Duct Tape
Letter Jacket

Can't afford to purchase a high school letter jacket? Duct tape the sleeves of any old jacket into that leather-sleeve look, then create your school's letter from matching or contrasting colors of duct tape.

Exfoliate with Duct Tape

Skip those expensive body creams and loofah scrubbers. Remove dead, damaged skin simply by pressing duct tape firmly into place and giving it a good rip. Mark our words, this will soon become a highly fashionable technique at the most respected spas in the world.

Art Censorship

Don't let them cancel your controversial art exhibit. Secure well-placed strips of duct tape to any parts that might be considered offensive and ensure safe viewing for the entire family!

"Look, Tim, your butt crack is showing!"

License Framer

No need to advertise your car dealer after you paid them so much for your car. Cover up the dealer's name on the license frame with duct tape and

advertise
your love
of duct tape
instead.

No More Bagging

Make yourself some grass clipping
retrieval shoes. Take an old pair of
snowshoes and cover them with
duct tape, sticky-side-out. Wear these
when you walk behind your mower
and you'll be picking up all the grass
clippings. Add new tape about every
four rows.

*Added benefit: By the time you finish your lawn,
you'll be a foot taller!*

Home Field Advantage

Football players: Duct tape your yard lines with white duct tape, sticky-side-up, and don't tell the other team. If your team can remember not to step on the sticky yard lines, you will truly have the home field advantage!

Airline Liquor Keeper

At $4 or more for one of those tiny little airline booze bottles, you can't afford to spill a drop of your in-flight cocktail. Duct tape your glass to the fold-down tray and ride out even the roughest turbulence spill-free!

Note: Be sure to ask for a straw.

Avoid "Shrimp Fingers"

A big problem when eating shrimp cocktail is that your fingers get saturated with that shrimp smell from holding on to the tail. Do what we do: wrap each little shrimp tail in duct tape. It not only looks classier than those pale pink tails, but it keeps that hideous smell off your fingertips.

"Wing Tips"

Retro fashion tip: Duct tape live birds onto your shoes to make your own pair of flashy "wing tips."*

Not endorsed by the ASPCA.

De-Inking with Duct Tape

Still using a typewriter? Clean your typewriter keys with ease: duct tape the carriage roller sticky-side-out, then strike each key until they're all ink-free.

The Duct Tape Sketchbook

Muzzle your Mutt

You may need to tape a straw in your dog's mouth to allow for drinking on hot days.*

*This hint is not endorsed by the ASPCA.

Shatter Sucker

Drop a plate that shatters into a zillion little pieces? Duct tape a yardstick, sticky-side-out, and drag it across the floor. The little pieces will be up in no time! Then placing duct tape sticky-side-up on your kitchen counter will allow you to reassemble the plate and give it a new tough gray coating at the same time.

Super Plug Plunger

Clogged plumbing? Remove the toilet plunger handle and drill a hole into the plunger. Now, duct tape your wet/dry vac hose onto the plunger where the handle was. Place the cup of the plunger firmly over the clogged drain. Reverse the airflow on your wet/dry vac and blow your drains clear!

< to Shop Vac

Convenient Mini Duct Tape Dispenser

Don't throw away your old credit cards. Wrap them with a few yards of duct tape so you can always have the Universal Power Tool handy in your pocket or purse.

Body Taping

No more dangerous body piercing to be stylish! Do what Jim and Tim do — body tape! Little folded-over pieces of duct tape on earlobes and eyebrows  and in the navel make the statement you're looking for without the risk of infection.

McDuctTape Burger

New!

Keeps the Insides Inside the Bun Until the Insides Get Inside Your Insides!

"Whenever we eat, we eat McDuctTape Burgers."
"Yeah."

– The Duct Tape Guys

Ceiling Lamp

Turn any lamp into a ceiling lamp. Just duct tape it to the ceiling.

Ceiling Fan

Turn any fan into a ceiling fan. Just duct tape it to the ceiling.

Ceiling Chair

Turn any chair upside-down and duct tape it to the ceiling. It will make people wonder what's up.

Asbestos Removal

When removing asbestos, do what the pros do: seal the openings of your protective clothing with duct tape.

"Hey, Jim, the hints on these two pages aren't funny . . . isn't this supposed to be a humor book?"

"Duct tape is a serious tool, Tim. I think we ought to be discussing some of its lifesaving attributes, too."

"You're right, as usual . . . I mean, you're right, this one time, Jim."

EB Green

The navy has a version of duct tape called EB Green. It's about forty times the cost of regular duct tape, but it's also the strongest stuff on the face of the earth. One single wrap of it has been known to patch high-pressure hydraulic lines up to 2000psi.

"Hey, Jim . . . I think I went to high school with Eb Green."

Hose-Off Flower Arrangements

Fake flower bouquets made out of different colors of duct tape brighten any room. They stay fresh forever, and when they get dusty, you simply spray them off with a garden hose.

Duct Tape Swimmees

Learning how to swim? Duct tape a couple of sealed bags of snack chips to your arms for use as flotation devices.

Bonus: If you get lost at sea, you'll have something to eat once you've learned to tread water.

Pest-Free Pooch

Keep those nasty fleas and ticks from infesting your poor little puppy. Encase your canine in a layer of fresh duct tape. Your pet will look quite handsome and be flea-, tick-, and burr-free all summer long.*

*Not endorsed by the ASPCA.

Tidy Garage

Prevent oil stains by covering the entire garage floor with duct tape. It provides a shiny new finish, too!

Or, encase your vehicle entirely in duct tape. This way you can keep the elements off your car, park outside, and use your garage to hold all your stuff.

Hot-Air Balloon

Use duct tape to patch your hot-air balloon — or to add an additional room or two to that little gondola basket.

"Use this hint at your own risk. Neither Jim or me has ever been in a hot-air balloon, let alone know about the laws of aerodynamics and thermo-rise-ology and technical stuff like that."

"But, Tim, you obviously know plenty about hot air!"

"Yeah. Just being around you, Jim!"

Here's a Boring Idea

Duct tape and your power drill can turn that old guillotine from a useless relic of the French Revolution into a fully functional drill press.

"Boring ... drill ... bore-ing ... get it, Tim?"

"Yeah, Jim, I got it the first time."

A Valid Excuse for Speeding

Next time the highway patrol pulls you over for speeding, tell the officer that your accelerator was stuck to the floor, then reach down and reveal your evidence: a wadded-up ball of duct tape (see page 48).

Cutting-Edge Office Accessories

1. Duct tape your old hedge clippers to the side of your desk so that one blade is stationary and flush with the tabletop: paper cutter.
2. Duct tape your electric hedge clippers across the top of a waste-basket: paper shredder.

Mulch On, Dude!

Turn any mower into a mulching lawn mower! Use duct tape to cover the exit chute. The grass and leaves will mulch and drop to the ground under the mower.

Fashionable Frock Fastening

Tired of constantly losing shirt buttons? Avoid the hassle by removing all the buttons before you even wear the shirt. Then keep it closed with a fashionable strip of duct tape.

You'll hear comments like: "Sir, is that a new shirt? It's so attractive. Very distinctive styling."

"Thank you, complete stranger. No, this is just an old shirt that I added duct tape to."

Camper's Companion

1. Pitch a tent using duct tape as ropes.
2. Patch a tent.
3. Make a tent (multiple rolls of duct tape are needed to create duct tape sheeting).
4. Hang your food out of bears' reach.
5. Repair a canoe.
6. Secure extra stuff to your backpack.
7. Plug your air mattress.
8. Bandage your flesh wounds.
9. Insect and pest control (see page 436).
11. Duct tape a "toilet sling" between two trees.

(Top 10 lists are too trendy, so we did 11.)

Sober Up

Friends don't let friends drive drunk. They duct tape them to the barstool until they sober up.

This hint has been sponsored by:

Office Joker

Come in early and duct tape the middle drawers of your coworkers' desks shut. One long strip along the back edge of the drawer attached to the underside of the desktop will usually hold the drawer tight.

"Don't forget to punch in so you get paid overtime for your little prank."

"Good thinking, Tim."

Prevent Faucet Freeze-Up

Folks in northern climates can wrap newspaper and duct tape around their outdoor water faucets to prevent freezing in the winter.

"But if you want a neat 'Ice Tube Dispenser' on the side of your house, don't do this hint."

"Yeah."

Harmonica Harmony

Duct tape two harmonicas together and you have one of those fancy chromatic harmonicas.

Duct tape two harmonica players named Phil together and you have the Phil Harmonica Orchestra.

See Tim's Harmonicarp on page 205.

Golfing with Duct Tape

Jim, an average avid golfer, offers these hints for using duct tape to improve your game:

1. Stop duffing shots because you can't keep your head down. Use duct tape to connect your forehead to your shorts and your noggin will stay in place.

2. Cover the face of your golf club with duct tape. When you hit the ball, you'll see an indentation where the ball is contacting the club face. Correct your swing accordingly.

3. Any shoe can be turned into a golf shoe. Just punch small nails through the sticky side of strips of duct tape, then adhere the tape to the bottom of your shoe.

Vacation Reminder

Mark your vacation days on your calendar with a strip of duct tape. If you're retired, cover your entire calendar with duct tape — you're on permanent vacation!

The Duct Tape Sketchbook

Can't afford the vet? Duct tape makes an excellent chastity belt.*

*Not endorsed by the ASPCA.

Crud Remover

Clean crumbs, spilled cereal, rice, dried bugs, etc. from your cupboards, countertop corners, and other tight spots by dabbing the stuff up with the end of a wooden spoon handle wrapped with duct tape sticky-side-out.

"Jim, you have some crud on your jacket. Here, let me remove it with my Crud Remover."

"Thanks, Tim."

Plastic Surgeon on a Roll

If you think your nose is too big, simply build up your cheeks, chin, and forehead with duct tape. You'll look correctly proportioned in no time.

Three-Legged Race

Don't let the current unavailability of gunny sacks prevent your company picnic from having three-legged races. Just use duct tape to connect the contestants' legs together.

"Yeah, just make sure you don't get Tim as a partner!"

"I hopped the best I could!"

"You were facing the wrong way!"

the DUCT TAPE GUYS™

Stuff from our Secret Recipe File

1 bike
+ 1 canoe
+ 14 mini paddles
+ duct tape
─────────────
= paddle boat!

Life jacket highly recommended

Ditch Jury Duty

Get out of jury duty by:

1. Duct taping two dozen egg cartons to your jacket.
2. Duct taping antlers to your head.
3. Hopping in bound and gagged with duct tape.
4. Or, show up wearin' nothin' but a duct tape loincloth!*

Warning: Hint 4, although quite effective, hurts like the dickens to remove.

Lopsided Tan Correction

If driving all day in the summer sun leaves you with a left-arm tan (right arm for you Brits), even it out by duct taping a battery operated sunlamp to the car ceiling so it shines on your shaded arm.

Stop Telemarketers

Duct tape your telephone to the hand set so you won't be tempted to answer during your dinner hour. You *know* it's just a telemarketer.

Lower Your Receding Hairline II

Make big, tall, Groucho Marx–like eyebrows out of duct tape to give the illusion of a lower hairline.

Cautionary advice: Really bald guys should avoid making their fake eyebrows too tall. This tends to look like racing stripes.

Roller Skis

Want to cross-country ski, but it's summertime and you can't afford those fancy roller skis? Simply duct tape four little toy trucks to the bottom of your snow skis and hit the road, Jack (or Jill)!

"But don't fall down, or you'll break your crown!"

"That's lame, Jim."

Stretch Your Sandpaper

Before attaching a sheet of sandpaper to your power sander, cover the back of the sheet with duct tape. Your sandpaper will last a lot longer. Or, avoid the need for sanding by entirely covering your lumber with duct tape.

Sheet Metal Workers:

1. Clean your metal file. Place a strip of duct tape over each side of your metal file and peel off the excess metal shavings.

2. Duct tape over sharp edges to prevent cuts while handling material.

3. Duct tape over your gashes when you forget to use hint 2.

Two small hand mirrors, two empty toilet-paper rolls, one empty paper-towel roll, and some duct tape makes a nifty little periscope!

Duct Tape Depth Finder

Find the depth of
a lake by attaching a
rock to the end of a
strip of duct tape on
a roll. Then unwind the
tape until the rock hits
the bottom of the lake.

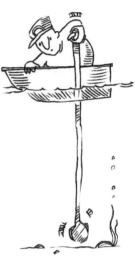

Make a Cold Pack

Soak a sponge in water and then
freeze it. Wrap the frozen sponge
in duct tape. Tape it to your aches.
When it thaws, simply stick it back
into the freezer. No need to resoak
your Cold Pack.

Private Parking

Create your own official parking spot
sign with black duct tape letters on the
side of a building. Or, duct tape over
the boss's parking sign and write in
your own name.

*Note: If you used our tape-over-the-boss's-parking-
sign hint, you may like to know that duct tape
also comes in handy when making* WILL WORK FOR
FOOD *signs.*

Trixie's
NEW! IMPROVED!
Tape-O-Suction™ Emporium

- Lose inches fast
- No dieting
- Expertly applied
- Almost patented technique
- Results guaranteed*
- 100% American Duct Tape

• *Call for a FREE consultation TODAY*

Before

555-WRAP

*After**

Individual results may vary. Not responsible for rashes and other skin irritations.

Trixie Sez: The Duct Tape Guys recommend our "Full-Service" Treatment!

we recommend Trixie's
"Full-Service" Treatment!
— Jim and Tim

Gals' Duct Tape Use

Put an end to that age-old argument: duct tape the toilet seat down.

Floatable Feast

Make your own pontoon boat: take
four empty 55-gallon drums, a picnic
table, an outboard motor, and lots
of duct tape, and you've got one
inexpensive pontoon picnic craft.

Do-It-Yourself Jacuzzi

Duct tape the hose of your wet/dry vac under the waterline of your bathtub and switch it on "reverse" to create an instant whirlpool!

Warning: Electrocution hazard!

Sewing Kit Organizer

Organize your sewing kit: a strip of duct tape sticky-side-out inside the lid holds all your pins and needles.

"Of course, if you're like us, and we know we are, you just hem and mend with duct tape."

Secure a Position

Who needs a winning résumé when a little bit of duct tape can get you the job of your dreams? Duct tape yourself to the human resource manager's desk until you hear "you're hired!" (or until you are introduced to members of the security staff).

Walk on Ceilings

Wrap duct tape around your feet, sticky-side-out, and walk up walls and across your ceiling.

Warning: Not recommended for people who weigh over 20 pounds.

Ouch!

That hurt!

Geography Students:

Take a map, a beach ball, and some duct tape, and you have yourself a globe.

"Hey, Tim, I have an idea."

"What's that, Jim?"

"Deflate the beach ball globe and you'll be able to get from North America to China more quickly by just punching a little hole through the ball."

"I'm concerned that that makes sense to me, Jim."

stump the DUCT TAPE GUYS

Question: *I currently have the flu. How can I use duct tape to get rid of it?* — *Sick in Bed*

Answer: We're no medical experts, but when Jim or I have the flu, we duct tape over both ends and go to work as usual. — *The Duct Tape Guys*

E-mail your questions to:
tim@ducttapeguys.com

Locksmith Bill Preventer

Prevent someone from accidentally locking a door by duct taping over the locking device.

Avoid Computer Eyestrain

Staring at a computer all day can be very hard on your eyes. Place a duct tape patch over one eye for 20 minutes, then switch the patch to the other eye for 20 minutes. This gives each eye some precious rest while you continue to work.

Warning: Not recommended when depth perception is required.

Quiet Your Soles

Tap dancers: Stop drawing so much attention to yourselves! Put a few layers of duct tape over those clicky things on the bottom of your shoes.

"I think they're trying to make all that noise, Jim."

"Well, that's the stupidest thing I've ever heard. If they want to make noise, why don't they just duct tape a bunch of pots and pans to their outfits?"

"Good idea, Jim!"

Central Vac

Always wanted one of those central vacuum cleaning systems for your house, but couldn't afford one? Duct tape flexible dryer tubing to your furnace vents and reverse the polarity on your blower so it sucks instead of blows.

Big-City Advertising on a Small Budget

Create mini billboards all over the city by duct taping your business cards everywhere. (You can also duct tape them to people's backs for walking billboards.)

the DUCT TAPE GUYS™

Stuff from our Secret Recipe File

1 lawn chair
+ 8 electric fans
+ 1 long extension cord
+ 1 roll Duct Tape
——————————————
= ultralight helicopter

Caution: Electrocution hazard

Talk Like a Duct Tape Pro!

Work these simple sentences into your everyday conversation:

"Duct tape: It's not just for ducts anymore."

"Duct tape: Don't leave home without it!"

"D'ya duct tape that yourself?"

"Duct tape changed my life.".............

"I'm wearing duct tape."

"It'd be cheaper to duct tape it."

Then try these:

"My name is [your name],* and I'm addicted to duct tape."

"Hey, pass the duct tape."

"Spare the duct tape and spoil the job!"

"If at first you don't succeed, duct tape it!"

and our favorite:

"It ain't broke, it just lacks duct tape!"

*Once again, don't say, "your name," just insert your name into this sentence. For instance: "My name is Tim, and I'm addicted to duct tape." Or, if your name is Bulah (let's hope it isn't), you'll say, "My name is Bulah, and I'm addicted to duct tape."

Easy Three-Step Furnace Duct Cleaning

1. Wrap duct tape, sticky-side-out, around a small dog.
2. Remove a heat vent cover.
3. Toss the dog's favorite ball into the open vent.
3. Yell, "Fetch!"

"Jim, you have three twice!"

"No one wants four easy steps, Tim."

Seasoning Saver

Clean up salt and pepper spills by
dabbing them up with duct tape.
In moist weather, cover salt shaker
holes with a piece of duct tape to
avoid clogs.

Bucket Stilts

Avoid the hassle of moving ladders around when painting or drywalling the ceiling. Duct tape two upside-down plastic buckets to the bottom of your feet for worksite stilts.

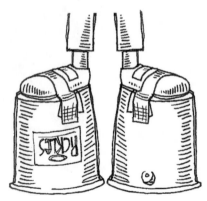

Deer Deterrent

Don't rely on those little "silent whistle" things to prevent deer from bounding into your car. Duct tape a decoy shaped like one of their natural predators — a wolf or a hunter — onto the hood of your car.

Mime Enhancer

Mimes: Duct tape a megaphone to your face so we can hear you!

Another mime hint: When you're pretending to pull an invisible rope, pretend to pull on invisible duct tape. Your little act will suddenly be more appealing.

Unicycling Made Easy

Learning to ride the unicycle? Duct tape yourself to the seat so you won't be so tempted to give up. You'll be up (and down, and back up) and riding in no time!

You Can Almost Smell the Ocean Air!

Create authentic, stereophonic ocean sounds by duct taping a conch shell to each ear.

Warning: Make sure the sand crabs are emptied out of the shells before securing them over your ears.

MSG on a Roll

Dry off your tongue as thoroughly as possible. Now press a strip of duct tape onto your dried tongue. Wait for your tongue and the duct tape to bond — about 60 seconds. Then, yank off the strip. Your tongue (and its taste buds) will be sensitized to bring out the flavor in any food. It's like chemical-free MSG on a roll!

Weave Me Alone!

Turn any chain-link fence into a privacy fence. Weave strips of duct tape between the links.

"Hey, Tim. Who's writing these stupid headlines?"

"I am, Jim. Why?"

"Oh . . . um . . . they're really quite clever. Good job!"

Enhance Your Lawn Furnishings

1. Replace or reinforce your aluminum lawn chair webbing with duct tape.
2. Duct tape a couple of old tires to each side of a chair to create a rocking chair.
3. Duct tape plastic butter tubs to the chair arms to make beverage holders.
4. Duct tape an umbrella to the back of your chair for sun and rain protection.
5. Tape two chairs side-by-side to make a love seat.

stump the DUCT TAPE GUYS

Question: *My friend Rod was behind my snowmobile riding on a car hood that I was towing. We rounded a corner and bam!! He hit a parked hay baler. We were moving at 55 or 60 miles an hour. Is there a way that duct tape could have prevented such a horrific scene? — Wahookiller@ . . .*

Answer: Well, duct tape can't prevent you from being stupid (it still hasn't helped Jim and me), but I guess you could take two car hoods and sandwich your friend (wrapped in foam rubber) between them. Duct tape around the hoods, and go for it! When he does happen to hit something, you'll need the Jaws of Life to remove him, but he will probably still be in one piece.
— The Duct Tape Guys

E-mail your questions to: tim@ducttapeguys.com

Shoelace tip Tip:
Duct tape around frayed
shoelace ends to make lacing
easy and to add a touch of
class to your old shoes.

Budget Laser Tag

Grab a buddy and make duct tape targets on your chests, then fling little sticky wadded-up duct tape balls at each other. It's budget laser tag! If you really want the visual effect of lasers flying through the air, use red duct tape.

Refinish Wooden Floors

Hold a dance in your house and duct tape sandpaper sheets to your guests' feet. When the evening is over, your floors will be beautifully sanded and ready to refinish.

Variation: Duct tape power sanders to your guests' feet and hold a life-size indoor electronic football game.

Romance Novel Models

Keep your bodices from ripping: duct tape all the seams before your next cover photo shoot.

"I think they're supposed to look like that, Tim, it makes them look passionate."

"Heck, if they want to look passionate, all they have to do is gaze upon a roll of duct tape!"

Air-Conditioner Draft Dodger

Air conditioner too small for your window? Use duct tape to seal any air gaps between the machine and the window frame (also helps hold it in place).

Note: If the air conditioner is too big for your window, bring it over to Jim's house. His just broke.

Energy Saver

Save on energy costs: duct tape over switches to keep them in the "off" position.

Travel Toilet Hygiene

Are you going to trust your hygiene to those flimsy tissue toilet-seat covers? Heck no! Do what we do: before you travel anywhere, cover your entire backside with duct tape! You'll be safe and sanitary for the whole trip.

Chimney Cleaning

Place a raccoon and a squirrel in a burlap bag covered with duct tape, sticky-side-out. Attach a duct tape rope and slowly lower the bag down your flue. The squirming action of the animals assisted by the bag's sticky exterior will get your chimney clean in no time.*

*Many of our hints have not yet been approved by the ASPCA. Please check with your local chapter.

No More Frayed Ends

Before cutting rope, wrap duct tape around the area that you're planning to cut. It will stop the rope ends from fraying.

"Hey, Jim, we should try that on your head before we cut your hair — maybe it won't get so frizzy."

"I don't think so, Tim."

"You ripped that line off Al!"

Stupid Pet Tricks Training

Secure a pork chop from a tree branch, just out of your dog's reach. This will teach it some valuable jumping skills. Keep raising the chop and your pooch will be on Letterman in no time.

Happy Hour Helper

Duct tape your two-for-one drinks
into one easy-to-hold glass.

Duct Tape for Better Bowling

Duct tape your hand onto your bowling ball. When you go down the alley *with* your ball, you'll have your 300 game quicker than you can say, "Get me another beer."

To tan under your chin, just cover a paper plate with duct tape, cut a hole for your neck, Slip it in place, Secure with duct tape tabs, and go Sun yourself.

A Bigger Haul from Santa

Extend and reinforce your Christmas stocking with duct tape to get a larger haul from Santa.

Tim's Christmas Stocking illustration (continued in our next book)

Convert-a-Bike

If your son refuses your daughter's hand-me-down bicycle because it has a dropped center bar, simply duct tape a broomstick in place and cover it with duct tape. Presto! A boy's model.

"Hey, Tim. Why did we skip from page number 318 to page 719?"

"I just wanted to see what it would look like if we had written a book over 700 pages long."

"Oh."

Clean Your Pores

Don't waste money on those expensive adhesive pore-cleaning strips. A strip of duct tape will do the job.

"Hey, Jim, what happened to your nose?"

"Oh, I left the duct tape on too long. Do you think it will grow back?"

Edible Earmuffs

Protect your ears from the winter
cold and pack a snack at the same
time. Duct tape a couple of
cinnamon buns to your
ears. This hint also works
well as a Princess Leia
costume for your next
Star Wars party.

Fishing for Fortunes

When you visit someone's house, wrap one hand with duct tape, sticky-side-out, and fish around in the couch cushions for spare change. You just may come out with enough to pay for the gas you used getting to his/her house.

Yes, now YOU can eat like a Duct Tape Pro!

NOW YOU CAN EAT LIKE A DUCT TAPE PRO!

DUCT-O's

- They're gray!
- They look like duct tape rolls!
- They're crispy!
- They contain NO duct tape!
- Jim and Tim eat 'em!
- They're fortified!*

Ask Mom to buy some today!

*No actual nutritional value has yet been identified.

If Duct-O's are not currently available in your grocer's fine cereal section—please ask for them by name!

Wonder Bra on a Roll

Lift and separate, or lift and squish together as current fashion dictates. Duct tape also comes in handy with those strapless formals.

Parents: If you are uncomfortable having your kids read about body parts, just duct tape these two pages together. Sorry. — The Duct Tape Guys

Butt Enhancer

If you weren't fortunate enough to
be endowed with a shapely posterior,
duct tape a couple of half-inflated
playground balls to your buns.
It will not only look attractive
but also feel great!

Bike Tire Reinforcer

If you aren't going to use our hint on page 120, try this one: line the insides of your bike tires with duct tape, then reinstall your tires. They will gain durability and you'll go miles farther before a flat.

"I like our method better, Tim."

"Yeah, but some people just like driving on rubber tires."

Pant Protector

Bikers can duct tape around their chain-side cuff to keep it from getting stuck in the chain.

"Jim, remember when your cuff got stuck in the chain and you had to bring your bike into your high school prom with you?"

"Shut up, Tim! Now everybody knows!"

Dome Light Deflector

Duct tape over the front of your car's dome light to provide a reading light for passengers while being nonobtrusive to the driver.

Evelyn Wood: Eat Your Heart Out!

Read a book cover-to-cover in 30 seconds! Duct tape all of the inside pages together so you only have one page to read between the covers.

Vise on a Roll

Who needs a vise when you have duct tape around? Instead, duct tape your project right onto the workbench. Also, duct tape together two pieces of wood that need identical bandsaw cuts.

"Another practical hint, Tim!"

"Yep. Hey, Jim, hand me a roll of duct tape. I just accidentally cut my watchband with the bandsaw."

"At least you used the right kind of saw."

The Duct Tape Sketchbook

Snowmobilers: Cover your face masks with duct tape to prevent windburn. And those involved in desert sports can use this to prevent their faces from being eroded away by blowing sand.

Canoe Capers

Renting canoes can be costly when you return them all scratched up. To make sure you get your deposit back, cover the entire bottom of the canoe with duct tape. Simply remove the tape before you return the canoe.

Create-a-Kayak

Duct tape over the top of your canoe and cut a hole over the middle seat. Plus, make an authentic kayaking oar by duct taping two canoe paddles handle-to-handle.

Duct Tape Luminaries

Create more durable lawn luminaries
by covering the paper bags with
duct tape and punching little holes
in the sides of the bag to emit the
candlelight. Use gray, or your choice
of colored duct tape, depending on
the season.

"Hey, Tim, your front yard is on fire!"

Automatic Crunches

Work on those abs while you watch TV. Duct tape your remote control to your foot so you are forced to do sit-ups whenever you want to change the channel.

Phew!

Sport Court on a Roll

Turn your driveway into a basketball court with floor markings made with easily removable duct tape.

Bonus: If you're not so hot from the three-point line, move it in a couple of feet, then move it out little by little as your shot improves.

Cosmetic Dentistry with Duct Tape

Dry off your teeth and cover them with bright white duct tape for the Jim Carrey *Mask* look, or use silver duct tape and you'll look like that mean metal-mouth dude in the Bond movie.

"My favorite is yellow, for that Austin Powers look."

"I thought those were your natural teeth, Jim!"

Trotting Trouble

Horse losing a shoe? Duct tape will hold it onto the hoof until you can get to the farrier.

"I thought you were going to say something about how duct tape can help you when you have the trots."

"Shhhh! Some people are trying to eat while they're reading this, Jim!"

Time-Saver Footwear

Turn any pair of tie shoes into time-saving slip-ons by tying your shoes loosely, then covering the laces with duct tape.

"Jim! When did you learn to tie your shoes?"

"I didn't. I just made duct tape slip-ons!"

Mute Your Pager

Silence your pager when attending church, concerts, and theater events: duct tape over the speaker, then duct tape the pager to your ear so only you can hear the beeping.

Ten-Layer Chip Dip

Use duct tape as the tenth layer in
nine-layer dip — it keeps the flies
away!

Place strips of duct tape as the top layer

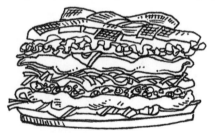

Toilet Seat Warmer

Toilet seat too cold? Duct tape a couple of hot water bottles to it to keep each cheek from freezing.

Or, duct tape Beanies* to your seat for a warm, fuzzy, cushioned seat.

*Not endorsed by Ty Inc., or any other bean-filled plush animal manufacturer.

stump the DUCT TAPE GUYS

Question: *Hey, Duct Tape Guys: My teenage son won't get out of bed in the morning. How can duct tape help? — Larry*

Answer: Larry, your son lacks motivation. Begin a father-son tradition of duct taping together. Start with something small — like that leaky plumbing under the kitchen sink. Progress to larger projects, like duct tape wallpaper borders in your workshop. Then start the ultimate duct tape project: converting your old car into a motor home using nothing but appliance boxes and duct tape. Soon your son will be beating you out of bed in the morning — especially when he realizes that the duct tape motor home will be a *great* babe magnet! — *The Duct Tape Guys*

E-mail your questions to: tim@ducttapeguys.com

45 Convertor

Vinyl records have made a big comeback for audio aficionados, but most have misplaced their 45 rpm inserts. No problem — just duct tape over the big hole and punch a little hole that will fit your turntable spindle.

We are pleased to present the Duct Tape Hair Club for Men with this complimentary ad in celebration of its 20th year in business. Here's hoping that we never have to become clients.
— Jim and Tim

Can't Lick This Idea

No more licking envelopes! A little square of duct tape seals the envelope flap — and looks like a Duct Tape Pro's version of one of those fancy sealing wax marks.

Homemade Pizza Cutter

Can't find the pizza cutter? Duct tape, two wooden spoons, a modified chopstick axle, and your *Best of Barry Manilow* CD combine to make a handy replacement.

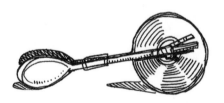

Sink Shower

Practical jokers: Cover the end of your sink faucet with duct tape. If you position the tape just right, the next person to turn on the faucet will get an unexpected shower.

Place duct tape here

A Cooler Cooler

When you hit the beaches during spring break, purchase a cheap Styrofoam cooler and cover it with two layers of duct tape. This way, the cooler lasts much longer (and with that silvery duct tape finish, it will attract the babes like crazy!).

All those fancy-pants art books have what they call color plates. Not to be outdone, our book features this page with a photo of a plate that you can color. — The Duct Tape Guys

EPA-Approved Fishing Sinkers

Concerned about lead from your sinkers leaching into the water while you're fishing? Replace them with little stones duct taped to your line.

"Is that really EPA approved now, Tim?"

"As far as you know, Jim."

Mock Pewter Plates

Duct tape both sides of your paper plates and magically transform them into a fine "pewterlike" service. Serve your guests with pride on these cheap yet elegant and unbreakable plates.

These plates are the perfect companions for the flatware described on page 106.

Camel Container

Going on a long bike ride? Carry your water with you! Duct tape a water-filled heavy-duty garbage bag to your back like a camel's hump. You can even duct tape fur onto it if you want that true camel look.

Caution: Shifting water in "the hump" caused Jim to end up in a cornfield during our test of this hint.

Picnicking Hints

1. Windproof your picnic tablecloth with a duct tape strip on each corner.
2. Or skip the tablecloth and cover the entire picnic table in duct tape for easier cleanup.
3. Put duct tape, sticky-side-up, around the perimeter of your picnic cloth to prevent ants from invading your lunch.
4. Seal and label your food containers with duct tape.

Keep on Your Toes

Cover the toes of thick socks with four or five layers of duct tape and you've got yourself some cheap and durable ballet shoes.

Deer-B-Gone

Do deer keep getting into your garden?
Lay duct tape, sticky-side-up, around the
perimeter of your garden. When deer step
on the tape, it will stick to their hooves and
legs and freak them out. Repeat for three
days and your problem
should be solved.

*"Tim, that's a stupid-looking
deer."*

*"Next time you get to
draw, Jim."*

Cat-B-Gone

Stop Kitty from lying on top of your refrigerator or favorite chair. Place a few strips of duct tape, sticky-side-up, where you don't want your cat to lie. The first time the cat tries to lie there with the tape in place will be the last time.

"Tim, how come we never did a Dog-B-Gone hint?

"Dogs, like duct tape, are a man's best friend. We'll leave that hint for lady Duct Tape Pros to come up with."

Tick Preventer

Camping or hiking? Prevent wood ticks from entering your clothing by duct taping your pant cuffs to your shoes. And a strip of duct tape, sticky-side-out, around your leg will prevent tick migration on the outside of your pants.

"Maybe if we put duct tape, sticky-side-up, on the country's borders, we could stop the immigration of illegal aliens."

"That's a good one, Jim. Send it to your senator."

Stay Put, Joey!

Kangaroo owners: Is your joey trying to leave Mom's pouch a bit prematurely? Just duct tape the pouch shut until it's time for the little roo to make its appearance.

Jim drew this

"So, Jim ... what is that, a dinosaur with a bumper?"

"Very funny, Tim."

This hint was actually used at the Wichita Zoo.

Do You Want Fries with That?

Next time you go to a fast-food drive-through, put duct tape over your mouth before you order — you'll sound just like the voice coming out of the speaker and they might be better able to understand what you're saying.

Pen Retainer

To keep your pens and pencils from rolling off your desk, attach a large, flat piece of duct tape.

"Prevent your coworkers from ripping off your pens by duct taping them to your hand."

"I gave that pen back to you, Jim!"

Sleepwalker Janitorial Service

Got sleepwalkers in your house? Duct tape their feet, sticky-side-out, so they vacuum for you as they walk around at night.

Note: We recommend duct taping only one foot. Otherwise, your roamers might get their feet stuck to each other and fall flat on their faces.

"Hey, Tim, did your wife's nose heal up yet?"

Fasten Fido's Food

Duct tape Fido's food dish to the floor so it doesn't end up on the other side of the kitchen after dinnertime.

Corn and Callus Remover

Duct tape an orbital sander upside-down to the floor and apply to your callused feet.

Warning: Don't fall asleep while sanding your feet. Tim couldn't walk without pain for a month!

Chia-Head

Cover your head with duct tape, sticky-side-out, and do headstands on a freshly mowed lawn.

No More Scorched Clothes

Duct tape the iron to your hand so you won't set the iron down and forget about it.

Warning: Watch out when you're wiping your nose.

Duct Tape Gift Wrap

Wrap your gifts entirely in duct tape for the gift that says, "Open me, eventually."

"Hey, Tim. Remember that gift you gave me for Christmas two years ago? What was in that?"

"Jim! You didn't open that yet?!"

"I've only made it through eight layers of duct tape so far. Can you give me a hint?"

"It's something wrapped in duct tape."

"Oh, thanks a lot!"

Tackless Tie Tack

Can't keep your tie from flailing all over your chest? Use duct tape as an invisible tie tack. Or, if you're a real Duct Tape Pro, duct tape around the entire tie and display your love of the tape.

Christmas Tree Skirt

Make your Christmas tree skirt out of red and green duct tape. Add a ring of sticky-side-up duct tape around the perimeter of the skirt to catch wayward needles.

By the way, wrap that inevitable gift of fruitcake in duct tape and use it as a durable and attractive doorstop.

Toy Noise Abatement

Did Grandpa and Grandma give your kid a toy that makes a hideously irritating sound? Join the crowd! Don't despair. Just duct tape over the speaker to muffle the volume.

Build your own "Snow Dome."
Just fill a glass with water.
Dump in some
glittery
snow stuff,
Duct tape an
Action figure
by its feet,
and insert it
into the water.
Seal the glass
with duct tape.
Invert for display.
Shake to make "snow" activate.

Less Whiffle, Faster Ball*

Kids: Cover the holes of a Whiffle Ball with duct tape and you'll get more speed on the ball when playing backyard baseball.

*This hint was used by Giants pitcher Russ Ortiz.

Avoid Potty-Mouth Pooch

Stop your dog from drinking the toilet water: duct tape the toilet lid closed.

Note: This hint can also be used by guys in retaliation for our "gal hint" on page 278.

Speaking of Which...

Hotel housekeepers: Save time cleaning toilets. Instead of wrapping the toilet seat and lid with that flimsy "sanitized for your protection" paper sleeve, seal it with duct tape. If guests can't get the toilet open, they can't get it dirty.

Shedding Solution

Has your dog's shedding problem turned your house into a furry mess? Wrap your

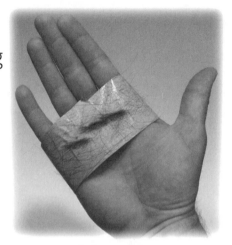

hand with duct tape, sticky-side-out, and enthusiastically pet your pooch until all the loose hair is removed.

Hair for the Hairless

Send the same duct tape that you used on your shedding dog to your balding friend. It makes a lovely toupee!

"Tim, it seems like we have a lot of hints for balding guys. Why is that?"

"Well, Jim, I think baldness is a topic that is on a lot of guy's heads."

"… I don't get it."

No More Ring Around the Collar

Apply a strip of appropriately colored duct tape to the inside of your shirt collar before you put the shirt on. At the end of the day, just rip out the strip and replace it with a new one.

Use a strip in each armpit and you may never have to wash your shirt again!

The Sticky Mentor Method

Having trouble learning a sport? Duct tape yourself to the nearest professional athlete. When it comes to learning, nothing beats hands-on experience.

Wart Remover

Duct tape placed firmly over warts for three or four days will destroy the malady for lack of oxygen.

"You know, Jim, this is another one of those actually true hints that really work. This one is even recommended by many doctors."

"Wow! Do you think we could get one of those 'four out of five doctors recommend' statements for our book advertisements, Tim?"

"No."

Speed Up Your Internet Connection

We've heard that "increased band width" will speed delivery of the Internet. So how about duct taping a bunch of phone cords together to create a wider cable to your computer?

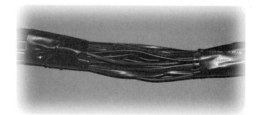

No More Postage

Want to save a stamp? Duct tape your letter to the back bumper of a bus going to your desired destination. Call the recipient and tell them to meet the bus at the station to remove the letter.

Platform Shoes

Make your own platform shoes just like those popular in the 1960s! Duct tape two bricks to the bottom of each shoe.

Added benefit: massive leg muscles!

Now Hear This!

Make a directional hearing aid: cut a Styrofoam cup in half from top to bottom. Duct tape one half over each ear with the open part of the cup facing forward. This will funnel sound right into your head.

Bonus spy hint: Face the cup opening backward to hear what people are saying behind your back.

Prevent Ugly Lawsuits

Cover the sharp tips of your chain-link fence so burglars can't sue you if they injure themselves sneaking into your yard.

"I thought you meant you were being sued for being ugly, Tim."

"Oh, good one, Jim!"

Duct Tape Gardener

1. If birds peck holes in your tomatoes, cover the holes with duct tape. The tomatoes will continue to ripen without rotting.
2. Duct tape your vine plants to stakes.
3. Duct tape tabs on a string about a foot off the ground around the perimeter of your garden to keep birds out.
4. Duct tape laid sticky-side-up on the ground around your garden keeps bunnies out.

Orthopedically Approved

Thanks to the many orthopedic surgeons who have validated this hint: Cover a cast with a plastic garbage bag, then securie it with duct tape so you can bathe while keeping the cast dry.

"I knew our ideas weren't all wet!"

"Good one, Jim."

Never Buy Gas Again

Save gas by duct taping your car to the bumper of another vehicle. Of course, the driver may get irritated at you for tailgating, and you're pretty much at his/her mercy as to where you can go.

"Hey, Tim. Why are we in Nebraska?"

"I guess I taped us to the wrong truck, Jim."

A Clever Costume

Here's a sticky idea for your next costume party: dress entirely in pink or minty green, and duct tape a shoe to your head. You're now a piece of used gum.

Jim-Proof/Child-Proof Your Kitchen

Use duct tape to seal your kitchen drawers, cabinets, and refrigerator and freezer doors. You can also put a strip of duct tape over electrical outlets to child-proof them.*

Make sure the duct tape you use does not contain any metal.

See Better Instantly

Distance vision failing you?
Skip that expensive
laser eye surgery.
Instead take
Polaroid photos of
what you're looking at
and duct tape them onto the brim of
your cap for a clearer image.

Tough Protection for Hands

Bricklayers, stained-glass artists, and clam shuckers alike can protect their hands from cuts by covering their fingers with duct tape.

"It's like glove on a roll, Tim."

"I couldn't have said it better myself, Jim."

"You probably would have added more words, Tim."

the DUCT TAPE GUYS™

Stuff from our Secret Recipe File

Jim & Tim's recipe for the perfect martini:

1. Cover sides of martini glass with duct tape.
2. Fill glass with beer.
3. Drink.
4. Repeat.

stump the DUCT TAPE GUYS

Question: *How can duct tape help me take the trash out to the curb at night? — Somaht O.*

Answer: Securely tape around your trash can and make a duct tape rope that extends across the street where the garbage truck will be passing in the morning. When the truck hits the duct tape rope, it will fling your trash can from the side of your house up into the truck, or possibly all over the street. Either way, duct tape has helped bring your trash can to the street for you. — *The Duct Tape Guys*

E-mail your questions to: tim@ducttapeguys.com

No More Floppy Ears

Turn your pet lop-eared rabbit into a regular bunny with a couple of Popsicle sticks and some duct tape.

"I think they're supposed to look that way, Jim."

"Oh, sorry. Disregard this hint."

Massage Chair

Get an old recliner, cut a slit in the back, remove all the stuffing, fill it full of squirrels, and duct tape the chair back together again. Cover the whole chair with a layer of duct tape to create a leatherlike feel and to prevent your back rubbers' claws from accidentally scratching you during your massage.

Note: Replacement squirrels may be required after a few days.

Run-Resistant Hosiery

Avoid runs in your nylons by covering them with duct tape. Nothing says "high fashion" like silver leggings. Looking for support hose? These things practically stand up on their own!

"Tim, what are you sitting on there?"

"Nothing, Jim! I'm wearing my duct tape support hose."

Make a Power Sander

1. Duct tape sandpaper onto one of your car's drive wheels.
2. Jack both drive wheels off the ground.
3. Start your engine and put the car in drive.
4. Hold the object you want to sand firmly against the spinning wheel that has the sandpaper on it.

Submarine Van Conversion

Fill six large, clear food-storage bags with water and goldfish. Duct tape the bags to the roof of your van so they hang in front of each of the windows. You'll actually feel like you're driving underwater in a submarine.

Coming Soon!

JIM & TIM
THE DUCT TAPE GUYS

ACTION FIGURES

More powerful than ordinary superheroes!
The Duct Tape Guys fight off the powers of
evil and broken stuff using only the
Ultimate Power Tool: duct tape!

from **DUCTCO** ™

We do hereby endorse these action figures as the
only authorized Duct Tape Guy action figures on the
market today (soon). All others are rip-offs.
Don't buy them! — Jim and Tim

Prevent Clawed Floors

Make little duct tape slippers for your dog or cat so its claws don't scratch the floor. Either that or duct tape entirely over your wooden floor for what we predict will be the floor covering of the future.

The Perfect Hostess Gift

Duct tape a bunch of used candle stumps together into one of those big multiwicked pillar candles that are so popular. Stick it in a roll of duct tape and you've created an attractive centerpiece — the gift that keeps on giving all year long!

Slimming with Duct Tape

Wrap duct tape around your torso (like a huge sticky girdle). It will slim you visually, at the same time that it makes you feel your girth more, causing you to want to eat less. This, coupled with the "sauna suit" aspects of the duct tape girdle, will work wonders on your figure in no time.

Bonus: Belly hair will be virtually nonexistent after using this device.

How to Program Your VCR in 5 Seconds

Cover that flashing 12:00 on your VCR with black duct tape and you will never have to learn to program your VCR. If you want it to display the correct time, duct tape a clock on top of the machine.

"Wow! That hint was worth the purchase price of this book alone, Tim!"

Burglar Deterrent

Before you leave on vacation, duct tape people shapes onto the insides of your window shades.
When the shades  are lowered and a timer turns on the lights it will look like your house is inhabited.

stump the DUCT TAPE GUYS

Question: I live on an island with a lot of trees and frequent heavy storms, so we frequently get power outages. When the power goes out, all the food in the refrigerator goes bad. How can duct tape help? — Christopher R.

Answer: During the next power outage, quickly put all your perishable food in a large cardboard box, seal the entire box in duct tape (it's waterproof), and attach a duct tape tether to one corner of the box. Now go off the island in a rowboat and dump the box into the cool waters surrounding the island. Sit in the boat holding the tether until the power comes back on. Haul the box aboard and carry your cold food back to your refrigerator. It's that simple! — The Duct Tape Guys

E-mail your questions to:
tim@ducttapeguys.com

Save Money

Wrap your wallet in a couple of layers of duct tape. It will cause you to think twice before making any impulse buys.

Baby Bowl Retainer

Does your toddler like to fling their food all over the floor? Just duct tape their dish into place and you'll get more food into him/her and less on the floor.

"Jim, this his/her gender thing is such a pain.

Let's coin a new term that's gender neutral."

"How about Duct Taper, or Ductee?"

"Keep workin' on it, Jim."

Create Your Own Weather Station

Adhere a rock to a strip of duct tape and hang it from a tree branch.

1. Rock hangs straight down: calm weather.
   a. Rock is wet: rain.
   b. Rock is white: snow.
2. Rock is moving slightly: calm breeze.
3. Rock is swinging back and forth: a storm is coming (seek shelter soon).
4. Rock and duct tape are parallel to the ground: storm is here (seek shelter now).
5. Rock is gone and duct tape is flapping wildly: tornado or hurricane (too late to seek shelter — duct tape yourself to tree).

Pocket Crumb Cleaner

Get crumbs, loose tobacco, sand, fuzz, etc. out of your pockets. Just wind some duct tape, sticky-side-out, around a pencil and dab it around in your pocket until it's clean.

The Duct Tape Sketchbook

Knowledge Magnet

Kids: Duct tape your head, sticky-side-out. This will help all that information your teacher throws at you to "stick" and soak into your head through a process similar to osmosis.

Do I Look Familiar?

Make yourself look instantly familiar to complete strangers. Duct tape a mirror to your face.

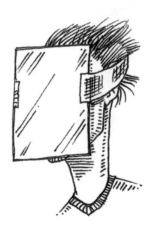

Pride in Patchwork

Make your own patchwork quilt with
no sewing experience! Cut up a bunch
of old flannel shirts into little shapes
and duct tape them onto a blanket.
Grandma would be so proud!

Black Belt

Become a karate black belt with little or no effort. Simply get a white bathrobe from your nearest fancy hotel and put a strip of black duct tape around the waist. Now walk the streets in the baddest part of town with complete confidence!

Cheap Burglar Alarm

Put duct tape, sticky-side-up, on a floor mat under each window and every doorway. When burglars enter the house, it will stop them in their tracks.

". . . Or at least cause the burglar to fall flat on their face! Why didn't you tell me that booby trap was there, Jim?"

"Sorry, Tim."

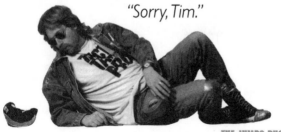

Cow Taping

A new-millennium twist to yesteryear's cow tipping: "Cow Taping." This kinder, gentler prank actually benefits the cows by keeping disease-spreading flies off them, protecting them from sunburn, and adding an attractive metallic sheen to their coats.*

*Not endorsed by the ASPCA.

Label Your Cows

Some are milking. Some are on medication. Which is which? Create a duct tape collar for the cows that are on meds and you'll easily keep the herd sorted.

This completes the "Cow Section" of our book. Now go drink some milk.

Poster Sticker-Upper

Duct tape not only holds your posters to the wall but also provides a nice frame for them.

Caution: Poster removal may have a tendency to bring the wall down with the tape.

Map Minder

Travelers can refold their road map to the section being used and duct tape it to the dashboard for easy reference. Then, to avoid the confusion of looking at all those unnecessary roads, duct tape over the entire map except for the route you'll be using.

"That idea alone is worth the price of this book, Tim!"

"Making this book worth twice the cover price!"

"Huh?"

Sidewalk Crack Sealer

Do your fellow citizens a favor: cover unsightly and potentially hazardous sidewalk cracks with duct tape. Either use gray, so it blends right into the cement, or a bright red or yellow to draw attention to the uneven surfaces.

"No more worries about your mother's back, either!"

Trickly Fountain Thing

Make one of those trendy little trickly fountains:

1. Duct tape a coffee can on top of a kettle.
2. Poke a hole in the side of the can.
3. Fill the can with water.
4. Sit down and enjoy the peaceful trickling sound.
5. Repeat from step 3.

Car Color Selection

When purchasing a vehicle, you should be willing to pay more for a silver-colored one. When you take into account the money you'll save by doing all your own bodywork with duct tape, you'll still be money ahead!

Get on TV!

Duct tape can help you get on one of those UFO sighting shows! Duct tape a cereal bowl upside down on a saucer. Cover the thing entirely in duct tape. Throw it up into the air and videotape it.

Before

After we videotaped it being tossed into the air

Lose a Lid?

If you lose a lid to a jar, duct tape over the opening will keep the food just as fresh for just as long.

Chicago residents: Avoid losing *your* lid — duct tape your hat to your head.

"Only in Chicago, Tim?"

"No, but Chicago is known as the Windy City, Jim."

"We'd better send them a case of duct tape."

Auto Bra on a Roll

Black duct tape over the front of your vehicle not only looks attractive but also protects your car's hood from stone chips and dings.

Do like we do — cover your entire car!

Temporary Trim Color

Remodeling an older house? Don't paint over that fine woodwork — subsequent owners might curse your very existence. Just duct tape over the woodwork to change its color. Not only will it dry instantly, but there'll be no messy paint-brushes to clean up!

Glacier Climbing Shoes

If your shoes are slipping while you climb on glaciers, just duct tape a couple of forks to the bottom of each shoe for extra grip.

Note: Any metal fork will do — just don't use those plastic "spork" things. They'll snap in half. It took us three hours to rescue Jim from that crevasse!

Drapery Tie-Backs

Nothing says "high-tech decor" like silvery duct tape drapery tie-backs. No hooks needed. Just stick the ends to the wall.

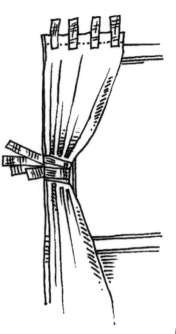

Fine European Lace*

Punch a lot of little holes in the shape of a flower into 10-inch strips of duct tape. Hang these strips from the top of your windows. There. You've made yourself a really durable lace valance.

*Sort of.

Easy Dusting

Got lots of knickknacks and collectibles? Then you know how time consuming it is to dust them all. But not when you duct tape them to their shelves and use a power blower to remove the dust!

Perma-Lunch Bag

Don't spend big bucks on a reusable nylon lunch bag for your kid. Make your own! Cover a paper lunch bag with duct tape and your kid will be the envy of the lunchroom. The bag will last all the way through college!

Go crazy and duct tape the inside of the bag, too!

Theater Prop on a Roll

No matter what your play needs in terms of props, costumes, or sets . . . you can probably make it out of duct tape. If not, you can enroll in Jim's and Tim's theater prop, set, and costuming class. (see ad on facing page).

Skaters' Dilemma

Wearing out the cuffs of your "skater pants" because you're constantly stepping on them? Either reinforce the cuffs with duct tape, or duct tape the pants higher up on your waistline.

Hands-Free Speaking

Turn any microphone into a lapel mike with duct tape. Wrap it tightly to your chest with a couple of rounds of duct tape.

Prevent Insect Intrusion

Avoid having spiders and other creepy things crawl into your mouth, nose, ears, and other bodily orifices at night — duct tape over all openings before you go to sleep. (Good luck breathing.)

Mini Pocket Protector

Don't want to look like a nerd with one of those pocket protectors, but don't care for leaky pen ink on your shirt either? Duct tape over the point of your pen until you're ready to use it. Or, duct tape the pen right to your hand so you're always ready to write.

Auto Air Control

Are your passengers always colder than you in the car? Duct tape over your heat vent, causing more heat to flow in their direction.

In the summer, reverse this hint when the air conditioner is on.

The "Jumbo" Hard Cover Version

Make this a hardcover book by duct taping a sheet of ¼-inch-thick plate steel to the front and back covers. It will last for years.

Jim — actual size

> That's not funny, Tim!

Dental Substitute

Lose a filling and can't afford to go to the dentist? You may have noticed that duct tape perfectly matches your old silver fillings. So when one inevitably pops out — just plug in a new one made of duct tape. No novocaine needed.

Pirates of the 21st Century

Pirates: Achieve the modern look in keeping with today's high-tech fashions. Make your eye patch out of duct tape. And while you're at it, cover your peg leg with duct tape; this way, you won't get splinters when you cross your legs.

Homemade Scream

With strips of duct tape, pull and stretch your skin into the horrid configuration of that *Scream* movie mask. Then go look in the mirror and scare yourself. A roll of duct tape is cheaper than going to see the movie — and you won't leave with that "I wasted eight bucks" feeling.

P·E·R·S·E·V·E·R·A·N·C·E

*With duct tape and a little
perseverance, you can turn
pyramids into… silver pyramids.*

Duct Tape

Duct Tape Snow Fort

Build a "snow fort" that will never melt. Cover a large appliance box entirely in white duct tape. It will last all summer.

Variation: Build a giant "sand castle": Cover a large appliance box entirely in duct tape, sticky-side-out, and throw sand on it. It will last all winter.

Space-Saver Suggestion

With enough cabinet space and duct tape, any kitchen appliance can become a space-saving under-the-cabinet appliance.

"Good in theory, Jim, but I think I just heard our refrigerator fall down."

Asleep on the Job?

Tape two strips of duct tape from your eyebrows over the top of your head and down your back. Stretch them tightly. The tension will keep your eyes open, your head upright, and pull on your back hair so you won't easily fall asleep. Even if you're able to doze off, you'll look wide awake and alert.

the DUCT TAPE GUYS™

Stuff from our Secret Recipe File

Campfire Gourmet Baked Beans

1 can Baked Beans
1 hot dog
1 roll duct tape
15 to 20 fast-food Mustard packets

Set can of beans in fire to heat. Dry off hot dog, wrap one end with duct tape, and leave 12-inch strip that you use to dangle hot dog over fire until dog heats up. Open can (HOT!), slice up hot dog using can lid, and mix in with beans. Add Mustard to taste. Enjoy!

Beernoculars

Football fans: Tired of having to put down your beer can so you can use your binoculars? Free up your hands by duct taping the binoculars to your face.

Hold the Starch

Sick of ironing? Duct tape over the wrinkles for a great look and a freshly starched feel. Remember, duct tape now comes in dazzling white, so you executives can make use of this time-saving hint, too!

Cheapo Greetings

Save those old greeting cards! Duct
tape over the original signature on
the card and you can resend it! Add a
small note that identifies the duct tape
strip as your "personal notary seal."

*Variation: Tape several cards together to make an
accordion-style greeting card.*

Buns of Steel, Duct Tape Style

Pants getting a bit too snug around your rear? Has your youthful posterior turned into "Buns of Tapioca"? Use duct tape to bind your bum into a firm and shapely mass.

"Hey, Jim. Why did you put a picture of me on this page?"

"Gee, I don't know…"

Duct Tape
Dream Catcher

Make a duct tape dream catcher
(modeled after those Native American
dream catchers). They catch dreams
like the dickens when they are made
out of sticky-side-out duct tape.

May all your duct tape dreams come true!
— Jim and Tim, The Duct Tape Guys

Index:

Visit The Duct Tape Guys' Web site
www.ducttapeguys.com
for updated hints, contests, duct tape apparel,
and other special announcements.

It's true!
Free Duct Tape!

You are entitled to a free sample roll of
Duck® brand Flat Pack™ Duck Tape®
Simply complete and mail this original coupon (no reproductions accepted) to: **Free Flat Pack™ Duck Tape® Offer**
P.O. Box #3599, Medina, OH 44256

Name: _____

Address: _____

City/State/Zip: _____

E-Mail: _____ Gender: M F Age: ____

This original Free Flat Pack offer form must be included with request and be postmarked on or before 10/31/01. Requests must be received by 11/30/01. Redemption expires 12/31/01. Limit of one free request/product per household. Allow 6 to 8 weeks for delivery. This offer may not be used with any other offer. Void where prohibited by law. Not responsible for any lost, delayed or illegible forms. Incomplete forms will not be acknowledged or returned. Exact FREE Flat Pack Duck Tape product is Manco item #03194.

The Duct Tape Guys wanna know...

Other than duct tape, what is your favorite household
tool/product? _____

If duct tape came in any other form other than a gray roll,
what would you want it to be? (Please describe.) _____

www.ducktapeclub.com

THE WIDE, WIDE WORLD OF
DUCK TAPE

Tear out this page and redeem for your FREE Duck® brand Tape!

TWO OUT OF TWO
DUCT TAPE PROS

Rip out
this page!
The other Side
has a
coupon
for a
FREE
Roll of
Duck® Brand
Tape!

It's true!
FREE
Duct Tape!

RECOMMEND
DUCK® Brand TAPE